# UNSOLV MURDERS

## TRUE CRIME CASES UNCOVERED

Written by
**Amber Hunt**
**Emily G. Thompson**

# CONTENTS

# THE SHROUDED HOUSE

**The residents of Villisca, Iowa thought of their little town as a friendly, neighbourly place. This illusion was shattered by a single, terrible event. Life in Villisca would never be the same again.**

It was a quiet Monday morning on 10 June 1912 in the farming town of Villisca, Iowa. A woman named Mary Peckham was bustling about, doing her chores, when she noticed an "odd stillness" at about 7:00 a.m. Normally by this time, Mary's neighbours would be bustling, too. Instead, aside from the impatient mooing of cows waiting to be milked in the field, their house was silent.

The house next door belonged to the Moore family – parents Josiah B. (a businessman known as either J.B. or Joe) and Sarah, and their four children: 11-year-old Herman, 9-year-old Katherine, 7-year-old Boyd and 5-year-old Paul. With that many kids, the home was rarely quiet. Worried, Mary called J.B.'s brother Ross, who used his key to get inside. He saw blood and asked her to fetch the town marshal.

## BLOODBATH

Marshal Henry "Hank" Horton was similarly shaken after walking through the silent house. "Somebody murdered in every bed," he muttered[1] as he went to fetch Dr J. Clark Cooper, the first physician to examine the scene. Inside the house, the entire Moore family had been

*Opposite page, main image:* The parlour bedroom in the Moores' house.
*Opposite page, clockwise from top:* Exterior of the Moore family house; a *Villisca Review* newspaper article on the murders; a sheet-covered mirror in the parlour bedroom.

8 VICTIMS

LAST VICTIMS OF MAD MURDERER OF WEST

J. W. Moore, wife and 3 of 4 children who were murdered in bed at Villisca, Ia. Star shows room in which Misses Stillinger, visiting Moores.

1 MURDER WEAPON | 7 KEY SUSPECTS

brutally slain, as had two young friends of the family, Lena and Ina Stillinger. The killer had wielded an axe, using the blade to kill his victims and then the handle to bludgeon their faces beyond recognition, before covering the heads with bedclothes. The mutilation was so severe that one Iowa newspaper misidentified the Stillinger girls as another pair altogether.

The night before the deaths, J.B. and Sarah were at the local Presbyterian church watching their children perform Children's Day exercises. Lena and Ina also took part, and the two girls – aged 11 and 8, respectively – were invited to stay the night at the Moore home. The young guests were in a downstairs bedroom, while the rest of the family was upstairs. Investigators determined Lena and Ina were the first victims – and that one of them had awakened, judging by a defensive wound that suggested she'd thrown up an arm to ward off a blow. It's possible that Sarah had also awoken during the attack. One neighbour told police she thought she heard Sarah's voice in the night yelling: "Oh! Dear! Oh! Dear! Don't! Don't! Don't!"

The Moore family were prosperous and **popular** in the area.

Lena and Ina were invited to stay with the Moore family because it seemed **safer** than having them walk home in the dark.

J.B. Moore received the **most blows** of all the victims.

# "ALL THE BODIES WERE FOUND IN A NATURAL SLEEPING POSTURE WITH HEADS BEATEN ALMOST TO A PULP."

ADAMS COUNTY FREE PRESS, 15 JUNE 1912

It appeared the killer had taken pains to conceal himself. The blinds had been tightly drawn closed on the windows. Glass doors had been covered with articles of clothing. Even the mirrors inside the house had been shrouded. The attack was not a robbery, as no valuables were taken or even disturbed. It seemed that the killer wasn't in a rush: he had taken time to partially clean the murder weapon before leaving it propped against the wall of the downstairs bedroom.

The crime scene had some odd elements that still perplex researchers today. A slab of bacon was left leaning against the wall next to the axe, while another piece of bacon was found on the

Police discovered two **cigarette butts** in the attic, implying that the killer or killers could have waited until the family were asleep before attacking them.

piano in the parlour. On the kitchen table was a plate of uneaten food and a bowl of bloody water. It's perhaps noteworthy, too, that Lena's nightgown had been pushed up, leaving her exposed – though doctors determined she had not been sexually assaulted.

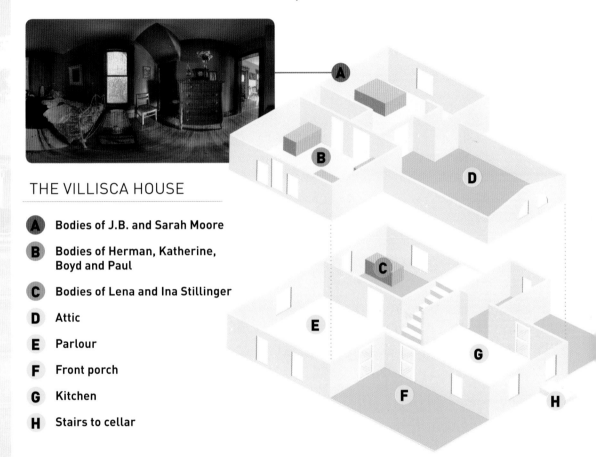

## THE VILLISCA HOUSE

**A**  Bodies of J.B. and Sarah Moore

**B**  Bodies of Herman, Katherine, Boyd and Paul

**C**  Bodies of Lena and Ina Stillinger

**D**  Attic

**E**  Parlour

**F**  Front porch

**G**  Kitchen

**H**  Stairs to cellar

## MURDER HOUSE CALLERS

About **100** people wandered through the house looking at the bodies before the Villisca National Guard arrived.

The police made a crucial error in failing to immediately secure the crime scene, allowing dozens of people to trample through the murder house. One suspect actually had a portion of skull in his possession that he bragged to several witnesses belonged to J.B. However, this man was able to plausibly explain he had simply picked up the piece of bone off the floor as he gawked.

The investigators' best guess was that the killer must have been a

9

relative of the family, and early reports tossed out some names: Samuel Moyer, a brother-in-law of J.B. and John Van Gilder, a former brother-in-law of Sarah. Townspeople racked their brains for clues and alerted police to every stranger they'd seen or bizarre scenario they'd witnessed. Many of the resulting "tips" ultimately proved useless.

May Van Gilder, the 16-year-old niece of J.B. and Sarah, said the Saturday before the murder, a stranger asked her where the Moores lived. When the girl later told Sarah of the query, Sarah reportedly replied that someone matching the description had been hanging around the home. That exchange prompted police to arrest a man in bloodstained shoes named Joe Ricks in Monmouth, Illinois. When May travelled to identify him, she said they had the wrong man.

Another dead end came when a supposed expert named C.M. Brown reached out to detectives and offered to obtain an image of the killer from the retina of Lena. The theory was that because Lena had awoken, the last sight she saw was the killer – and that image would be imprinted on her retina much like a photograph. Detectives agreed, and Brown said he recovered an image that "indicates a man of stout build, very broad shoulders, and extraordinary length between the shoulders and hips".[2] Unsurprisingly, nothing came of it.

**J.B.'s brother-in-law Samuel Moyer** was arrested but discounted because he had an alibi.

On the day of the murder, **several posses** of local people went out looking in barns and outbuildings, hoping to catch the killer.

**Photography** was making rapid advances in the early 20th century. Optography – obtaining an image from a dead person's retina – was thought a serious possibility.

# 9 June 1912 / Strangers spotted near the Moores' house.

However, some tips were more promising. Cora McCoy, who lived two blocks from the Moore house, said she saw two strangers walk by at about 3:00 p.m. on Sunday afternoon, the day before the murders. The men walked close together, as if talking confidentially. McCoy said she saw them again at dusk. One of them looked like a man named William "Blackie" Mansfield, a supposed Army deserter and "cocaine fiend" who, two years after the Villisca murders, was suspected in the similar axe slaying of his wife, daughter, father-in-law and mother-in-law.

Another neighbour of the Moore family, Mary Landers, also saw two strange men walking towards their house. She said they paused to look at Moore's axe, which was in a chopping block in the yard.

## CONSPIRACY THEORY

Several witnesses said that they spotted Iowa Senator Frank F. Jones and his son Albert in town at the time of the murders. On the surface, this might seem harmless, but J.B. had worked for the elder Jones' farming equipment company before leaving to start a competing business. Jones was reportedly upset by his departure – and by his nabbing of a lucrative John Deere contract. There were also rumours that J.B. was having an affair with Jones' daughter-in-law, Dona. It all made for bad blood – but was it enough to kill?

Local men Fred Fryer, Frank Milhiller and Verne Robinson all reported seeing J.B. talking with Sen. Jones' son a few hours before the murders. Another man, Jim Bridewell, said he saw Albert Jones with Villisca pool hall owner W.B. "Bert" McCaull. Garage owner E.M. Nelson said he spotted McCaull behaving suspiciously and in a rush about 9:00 p.m. on the night of the slayings, while several witnesses said McCaull had shown them a piece of bone that he said came from J.B.'s skull.

These witness statements led to theories that Sen. Jones, Albert Jones, Blackie Mansfield and Bert McCaull had worked together. A detective named James Wilkerson, who worked for the renowned Burns Detective Agency, was hired to investigate the killings after police came up empty-handed. In 1916 he announced he had solved it, stating that Sen. Jones had hired Mansfield to murder J.B. for hurting his business. The theory was bolstered by testimony from Alice Willard, a Villisca busybody recruited by Wilkerson to help investigate the case. Willard said that on the night of the murder, she and two other women had driven home from Lincoln, Nebraska, when their car broke down near the Moore house. As she reached the back corner of the Moore lot, she saw five men talking in hushed voices. While she couldn't hear much of their conversation, she said she picked out some key words and phrases: "money", "Sunday", "after church" and "get Joe first, the rest will be easy". She recognized one of the men as Sen. Jones.[3]

Wilkerson's claims were heralded with huge headlines: GREAT CRIME AT VILLISCA IS NOW SOLVED read one from Marshalltown, Iowa. The story claimed that Mansfield not only had been hired to kill

Modern forensic science would likely have solved the Villisca case. However, in 1912, even **fingerprinting** was still new, and law enforcement cooperation across state lines was poor at best.

Sen. Jones' **career was ruined** by the allegations, and he sued Wilkerson for slander. The senator lost the $60,000 defamation lawsuit.

After his acquittal, Blackie Mansfield successfully **sued** the Burns Detective Agency and Wilkerson for $2,250.

Some investigators ridiculed Willard's account, because she waited **four years** to share it. She explained she had been too afraid.

J.B. Moore, but he was also responsible for the double axe murders four days prior in Paola, Kansas. The allegations against Mansfield were brought before a grand jury, but Mansfield's employer provided records saying he had been in Illinois at the time of the murders. Mansfield was never charged. That didn't stop Ross Moore (J.B.'s brother) or Joe Stillinger (Lena and Ina's father) from believing Wilkerson's theory.[4]

On 6 June 1912, in Paola, Kansas, Rollin Hudson and his wife Ana were **murdered** while they slept. No motive was discovered and no one was charged.

## SERIAL AXE KILLER?

Neither Villisca nor the Paola killings were the only axe murders of the era. There was a string of similar killings throughout the Midwest, many of which were ascribed to Henry Lee Moore (no relation to the Moores of Villisca). Moore was found guilty of the murder of his mother and grandmother in December 1912, and US Department of Justice agent M.W. McClaughry theorised that he could be responsible for as many as 23 more – including the Villisca deaths.

McClaughry pointed to similarities beyond the murder weapon. Each victim was slain in their homes with exceptional brutality. In each case, the bloody axe was found nearby. He also noted that the axe murders started in late April 1911 and stopped in mid-December 1912 – a window of time during which Henry Moore was out of prison.

In their book, *The Man From the Train*[5], Bill James and Rachel McCarthy James claimed that Paul Mueller, a German immigrant farmhand, was a serial killer who travelled by train and killed families with their own axes. The Villisca slaying is one of many killings they pinned on this elusive character. Some townspeople said that they had spotted Mueller shortly before midnight on the night of the murders, and he seemed to be in a rush. After the bodies were discovered, a nationwide manhunt ensued, with Mueller reportedly holing up in Wisconsin, New York, Pennsylvania and beyond. He was never found.

The authors of *The Man From the Train* also assert that Mueller could have been responsible for the 1922 **Hinterkaifeck murders.**

## PEEPING TOM

One suspect was actually tried for the Villisca deaths. The morning the bodies were found, a reverend by the name of Lyn George Kelly left Villisca by train at about 5:20 a.m. On the train – long before the bodies had been discovered – he allegedly told fellow travellers that there were eight dead souls back in town who had been butchered in their beds. Word of this prompted investigators to take a close look at Kelly, who had arrived in town the morning of the murders and even attended the Children's Day in which the youngsters had performed.

Two weeks after the murders, Kelly returned to Villisca and posed as a detective, joining a tour of the murder house. He inserted himself further into the case by claiming that, at about 1 a.m., he had actually heard the thud of the axe that killed the eight victims.

Kelly had a history of mental illness and related odd behaviour. "He was schizophrenic, there was no doubt about that," said Ed Epperly, a PhD at Luther College in Decorah, Iowa, who studied the case for nearly 40 years. "I think (the motive) was sexual." Epperly points to the uplifted nightgown on one of the victims and draws a parallel between that and Kelly's habit of "window peeking". Kelly had also been charged twice with sending obscene materials in the mail, asking young girls to pose nude for him.

## A TOWN DIVIDED

In 1917, a grand jury heard evidence against Kelly and indicted him for the Villisca murders. As he awaited trial, Kelly even signed a confession to the murders, saying God had told him, "Suffer the little children to come unto me" and "slay, slay utterly".[6] However, Kelly recanted his confession at trial, and the jury deadlocked 11 to 1 for acquittal. A second jury acquitted Kelly in November 1917. The townsfolk in Villisca were split in their beliefs. Some residents thought Sen. Jones was the culprit, while others were convinced Kelly was the killer. "It really tore the community apart," said filmmaker Kelly Rundle, who made a movie about the murders called *Villisca: Living with a Mystery*.

The case has also acquired a supernatural aura. The Villisca house has been investigated by numerous "ghost hunters", who claim to have encountered paranormal phenomena, helping to make the building a tourist attraction. Visitors can even stay there overnight.

Kelly allegedly mailed a bundle of **blood-soaked clothing** to a laundry soon after the murders.

Kelly was the son and grandson of **English ministers**.

Epperly believes Wilkerson's conspiracy theory involving Sen. Jones had led the **jury astray**.

# A HOLLYWOOD WHODUNNIT

**It was a thriller plot fit for the movies: A famous film director mysteriously murdered in his home. For extra glamour, some of the suspects were genuine stars of the silver screen. For extra spice, William Desmond Taylor had a secret past...**

The name William Desmond Taylor is no longer familiar to modern moviegoers, but in the 1910s and 20s, he was a prolific director whose name routinely appeared in gossip columns alongside that of one beautiful actress or another. He worked with legends of the silent film era – Mary Pickford, Myrtle Stedman, and Wallace Reid – and lived in a stylish bungalow in a sought-after Los Angeles "movie colony" neighbourhood. To his Hollywood friends, William Desmond Taylor seemed to have it made.

Such was the case until the morning hours of 2 February 1922, when Taylor's valet and cook, Henry Peavey, found his lifeless body lying face-up on the floor of his study. Peavey ran screaming from the bungalow into the apartment building's courtyard. At first, it appeared that the 49-year-old director must have succumbed to natural causes. His suit was unmarked, said a neighbour, the actor Douglas MacLean, who rushed to William's home as soon as he heard Peavey's cries. "He was lying flat on his back, his feet separated a little, his hands at his side, perfectly flat on his back," MacLean commented. "I said to

*Opposite page, clockwise from left:* William Desmond Taylor; movie star Mabel Normand; Margaret Gibson, a.k.a. Patricia Palmer; Taylor's valet, Henry Peavey; Taylor's former valet, Edward F. Sands; Mary Miles Minter as Cleopatra; Charlotte Shelby (left) and daughter Mary Miles Minter, some 15 years after the murder.

1 VICTIM | 5 KEY SUSPECTS

Mrs. MacLean, later on, 'He looked just like a dummy in a department store, so perfect, so immaculate.'"[1]

Movie mogul Adolph Zukor, president of Famous Players-Lasky, Hollywood's preeminent studio, was desperate to hush up the potential scandal of Taylor's death. Before the police arrived, he sent employees around to Taylor's house to remove any bootleg liquor or compromising material. They also told Peavey to clean up the crime scene.

As soon as the police turned the dead man over, it was obvious that Taylor had not died a natural death. He was lying in a pool of blood, with a bullet wound in his back. From the angle of the wound, the gun had probably been fired by someone standing just over 1.5 metres (5 ft) tall, possibly while embracing Taylor.

William Desmond Taylor's murder would become one of Hollywood's darkest legends, with every twist and turn of the investigation lapped up by the press. Gossip peddlers could not have wished for better material.

The industry had recently suffered several **blows**, such as rape and murder charges against comedy star Roscoe "Fatty" Arbuckle, whose third trial loomed as Taylor lay dead.

**Robbery** clearly was not a motive: Taylor still had $78 in his wallet.

A reporter working for the *New York Daily News* attempted to **trick** Peavey into confessing to the murder.

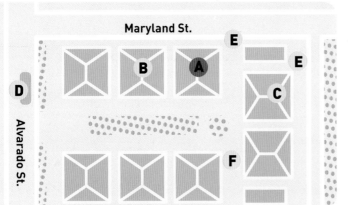

## ALVARADO COURT APARTMENTS

**A** 404B, W.D. Taylor
**B** 402A, Edna Purviance
**C** 406B, Douglas and Faith Mclean
**D** Mabel Normand's car
**E** Possible exits for murderer
**F** Faith Mclean sees man at 8:00 pm

## THE FIRST SUSPECT

Unfortunately for actress Mabel Normand, the police's inevitable first step was to suspect whoever last saw the victim. Considered one of the top comediennes of the era, Mabel had huge, expressive eyes, and dark hair, cropped flapper-style. By 1922, she was working for Goldwyn Studios for about $1,000 a week – the equivalent of nearly $15,000 today. She also had a drug and drinking problem; coincidentally, perhaps, Taylor was famously on a crusade to rid Hollywood of drugs.

Mabel Normand had worked alongside legends such as **Charlie Chaplin**, Harold Lloyd and the aforementioned Fatty Arbuckle.

# 1 February 1922 / Mabel Normand is the last known person to visit William Desmond Taylor at his home.

A **locket** with Mabel's picture and an inscription "To my Dearest" was found in Taylor's belongings.

In 1924, Mabel's name was once more linked to a murder. Her **chauffeur**, R.C. Greer, confessed to shooting wealthy oilman C.S. Dines.

In a 1930 interview in the *Los Angeles Record*, Peavy claimed that **Mabel Normand** was Taylor's murderer.

Normand denied knowing anything about the murder, claiming that her visit was completely innocent. Taylor had bought her a book and called her to pick it up. She arrived between 7:00 and 7:15 p.m.; they talked about literature and theatre; and then, after about half an hour together, he walked her to her car and they waved goodbye. "Please tell the public that I know nothing about this terrible happening and that Mr Taylor and I did not quarrel," she said in a press statement.[2]

After being repeatedly questioned, Mabel Normand was dismissed as an official suspect, though a cloud of suspicion remained over her. As recently as 1990, author Robert Giroux put forth a theory that William's determination to help Mabel beat a cocaine addiction angered her drug dealers, and so they killed him in revenge.

## A TEENAGE CRUSH

Search newspaper mentions of William Desmond Taylor in the months leading up to his death, and nearly every story includes the name of 19-year-old up-and-coming actress Mary Miles Minter. Born Juliet Reilly in 1902 in Shreveport, Louisiana, Mary was a doe-eyed beauty in the mold of Mary Pickford – though 10 years younger.

Taylor had directed Mary in the 1919 silent film, *Anne of Green Gables*, in which she played the title role, and he was known to be invested in her career. After his death, investigators found love letters from Mary among Taylor's effects. The notes were written in a silly code "known to thousands of youngsters", while one read "I'd put on something soft and flowing... I'd wake to find two strong arms and two dear lips pressed on mine in a long, sweet kiss".[3] This implied a far more intimate relationship than even Taylor's closest friends had realized. While Mary's mother tried to downplay her daughter's declarations, saying that Mary loved William "as a child would her father"[4], Mary herself said otherwise, referring to him as the love of her life.

# "I LOVED HIM DEEPLY... WITH ALL THE ADMIRATION AND RESPECT A YOUNG GIRL GIVES TO A MAN WITH HIS POISE AND UNFAILING CULTURE."

MARY MILES MINTER

Reporters latched onto Mary's romantic revelations, painting her as both virginal and a temptress – a young woman who mistook William's kindness as something more. No evidence surfaced that he ever returned Mary's love. After his death, the rumour was that he was actually gay or bisexual. One typically lurid story in the *New York Daily News* reported that William engaged in "unmanly rituals" as part of an opium cult.

Taylor and Minter's secret relationship was enough to warrant interrogation. The fact that she had no alibi, and that police believed three long blonde hairs found on Taylor's jacket were hers, helped to ensure her name would be forever linked to the case. In 1937, 15 years after the murder, police made it clear that Mary was still a prime suspect when they subpoenaed her, her mother and her sister, claiming they had uncovered "new evidence". Mary publicly demanded that the authorities should either clear her name or try her for murder. Neither ever happened.

## FATAL ATTRACTION

Nevertheless, Mary has remained a suspect. The writer Charles Higham suggested in his book, *Murder in Hollywood: Solving a Silent Screen Mystery*, that Mary was jealous of his affairs with other women and men[5]. Higham posits that, the night of the killing, Mary turned up at William's home with a gun and threatened to kill herself if he would not return her love. He calmed her down, but she was still holding the gun as they embraced and accidentally shot him.

As quickly as Mary Miles Minter's name hit the headlines as a possible suspect, so, too, did her mother's. Charlotte Shelby had been

Mary said she and Taylor had been **engaged**— a claim that was never corroborated.

A **pink nightgown** found in Taylor's home was reported to have Mary's initials on it. However, this was discredited.

Art director **George James Hopkins** – who went on to have a stellar Hollywood career – was in a relationship with Taylor when he was killed.

a Shakespearean actress who had appeared on Broadway in at least one production, but her stardom fell as she raised her two daughters – Mary and Margaret Fillmore. By some accounts, there was no love lost between Charlotte and William Desmond Taylor. Charlotte's former secretary told a district attorney attached to the case that she heard Charlotte tell Taylor, "If I ever see you hanging around my Mary again, I'll blow your goddamn brains out."

## THE MATRIARCH

On the surface, it would seem ludicrous to think Charlotte would want Taylor dead. He was, after all, shepherding her daughter's career, and thus helping the whole family financially. Some commentators posited that Charlotte was merely a protective mother trying to shield her young daughter from a man nearly three times her age. Mary herself rebuffed that notion: "Mother's actions over Mr Taylor's attentions to me were not inspired by a desire to protect me from him. She was really trying to shove me into the background so that she could monopolise his attentions and, if possible, his love."[6]

Even more damning were comments – and court testimony – provided by Charlotte's older daughter, Margaret. According to her, neither Mary nor Charlotte was home between 7:00 and 9:00 p.m. on the night of the murder. Mary eventually arrived in a "hysterical condition", while Charlotte did not come home at all."I knew she was out all day and night hunting for certain men to learn Mary's whereabouts... [She] later came in and told us that Taylor had died." Margaret told police that her mother had tossed "the gun" into a river in Kansas City. Soon after, Charlotte had Margaret committed to a psychiatric ward.

Beyond the daughters' incriminating statements about Charlotte's possible role in Taylor's death, police uncovered convincing circumstantial evidence against the matriarch. She allegedly owned both the type of gun, and the rare, soft-nosed ammunition used in the killing.[7] While this was not enough to convince a grand jury, it was plenty to convince Ed King, one of the lead investigators on the case, who went to his grave believing Charlotte Shelby got away with murder.

Both Mary and Margaret would publicly battle their **domineering mother** in separate court actions years after Taylor's death.

Charlotte Shelby created her daughter's stage name by having her take the identity of a **deceased cousin** – the real Mary Miles Minter. This was to make people believe that Juliet was older, and therefore allowed to work without being in violation of child labour laws.

## DOUBLE IDENTITIES

The list of suspects does not end with Charlotte Shelby. Suspicion also surrounds the dead man's chauffeur and his own brother. The roots of this theory lie in Taylor's early life – one he abandoned 14 years before his death. He was born in 1872, not as William Desmond Taylor, but William Cunningham Deane-Tanner. The eldest son of a wealthy landowner and the grandson of a member of parliament, William was raised in Mallow, Ireland, with a younger brother named Denis Gage Deane-Tanner. William longed to become an actor, and disappointed his family by refusing to join the army, joining a theatre group in Manchester instead. He bounced around the UK and then Canada, before landing in New York, where Denis joined him. The two opened an antique shop on Fifth Avenue.

In 1901, at the age of 29, William married Ethel Harrison, the niece of a real-estate tycoon, and the two had a daughter named Ethel Daisy. In 1908, William is said to have emptied his bank account and vanished, leaving no forwarding address for his wife and child. Ethel would eventually learn that her husband had moved to Hollywood when she and her daughter saw him on the silver screen using a new name.

Four years after William disappeared, so did his brother, Denis, in similar fashion. His wife said he left the house with his hat and walking stick, as though going to work, never to return. Neither his wife nor his two small children ever heard from him again.

Some time in 1920, Taylor hired a man named Edward Sands to be his chauffeur. A year before his murder, he and Sands had a falling-out. Taylor accused the chauffeur of stealing from him and threatened to have him arrested. Sands disappeared shortly before the shooting and was sought by police as a potential suspect.

This all serves as a backdrop to one of the more convoluted theories surrounding Taylor's death: That Denis had assumed the identity of Edward Sands and – after falling out with his more successful brother – had shot him. This theory even made the newspapers, as evidenced by a 1936 Associated Press story that asked: "Was the 'Edward Sands' who

Ethel was granted a **divorce** on charges of adultery four years after William left her.

Taylor reconnected with his **daughter** shortly before his death. She told reporters that her father's letters were filled with mentions of Mary Miles Minter.

Taylor's daughter inherited his entire estate (after debts were paid off), totaling nearly **$19,000** (over $270,000 in US dollars today).

presumably acted as his valet, really his brother, Dennis (sic)?" Denis' abandoned ex-wife, Ada, tried to clear his name, insisting that the brothers were "very much devoted to each other" and providing police with photos, documents, and handwriting samples. Neither Denis – nor Sands – ever resurfaced, however, so the conjecture continues.

## THE GIBSON GIRL

In 1964, 42 years after the elusive killer struck, a woman named Pat Lewis declared on her deathbed that she had killed William. On its own, this confession would not mean much – police claimed that the case had garnered some 300 confessions within the first six weeks of the investigation – but a family friend did some digging and found there was perhaps something to Pat Lewis' claims.

Lewis had once been known as Patricia Palmer and, before that, had achieved some movie-star fame as Margaret "Gibby" Gibson. By 1964, she was a recluse living in a small house in the Hollywood Hills. When she suffered a heart attack, she demanded a priest and began confessing her sins – namely that while she was a silent-screen actress, she had shot and killed William Desmond Taylor. "And she continued by saying that they nearly caught her and that she had to flee the country," wrote Raphael F. Long in a piece published by *Taylorology*, a newsletter dedicated to the murder.

Bruce Long, author of *William Desmond Taylor: A Dossier*, hypothesised in the same newsletter that Gibson had, like Mary, fallen in love with William – ultimately killing him in a "if I can't have him, no one can" frenzy.[8] William J. Mann, author of *Tinseltown: Murder, Morphine, and Madness at the Dawn of Hollywood*, suggests that the actress was trying to blackmail Taylor over the family he had abandoned and had recruited help from local crime boss, Blackie Madsen, and known blackmailer, Don Osborn. Mann posits that one of those men, rather than Gibson herself, pulled the trigger.

In movies, this compelling mystery would surely have a clear ending. However, it became clear long ago that the murder of William Desmond Taylor will never have a satisfying third act.

# THE BODIES IN THE BARN

**Few unsolved murders encompass so many dark secrets and raise so many disturbing questions as this lurid, spooky tale of incest, jealousy and mystery.**

Hinterkaifeck was the name of a small, isolated farmstead situated in the beautiful rolling hills and forests between the towns of Ingolstadt and Schrobenhausen in Bavaria, Germany. It was the home of Andreas Gruber, 63; his wife, Cäzilia, 72; their widowed daughter, Viktoria Gabriel, 35, and her children, Cäzilia, 7, and Josef, 2; and also the new maid, Maria Baumgartner, 44. In the dead of night, on 31 March 1922, someone systematically slaughtered each member of the family one by one and piled their bodies in a barn.

## THE GRUBER FAMILY

Andreas Gruber was not a popular man in the local commuinity. He was thought to be aggressive and greedy, and people in the nearby village generally avoided him. Viktoria was the only child of Andreas and Cäzilia to have survived into adulthood; locals speculated that their other children had perished because they were not looked after properly and were treated cruelly. "The small children had to stay in the cellar for days and when you passed by, you could hear the children crying," a neighbour recalled.

*Opposite page, main image:* A contemporary reconstruction of the crime scene.
*Opposite page, top to bottom:* Hinterkaifeck Farm, a few days after the crime. The barn, where the murders took place, is on the right; Maria Baumgartner's body in her bedroom; the bedroom where Viktoria slept with her two children; the crime scene, as first encountered by the police.

6 VICTIMS | 6 KEY SUSPECTS

Even more damaging to Andreas' reputation was the public knowledge that he was having an incestuous relationship with Viktoria, whose husband, Karl Gabriel, had died in France in 1914 during World War I. The year after his death, Andreas and Viktoria were convicted of incest between the years 1907 and 1910. Viktoria was sentenced to one month and Andreas to one year in prison. It was also rumoured that Andreas was the real father of little Josef and not the village mayor, Lorenz Schlittenbauer, with whom Viktoria had also been having an intimate relationship at the time she became pregnant. Lorenz had reportedly wanted to marry Viktoria, but he had been stopped by Andreas, who had angrily chased him away from the farm with a scythe. Kreszenz Rieger, the Gruber's maid before Maria Baumgartnerr, later told police that she had overheard Andreas telling Viktoria that "she does not need to marry, because as long as he lives, he is there for 'this'". The maid claimed that, by "this", Andreas was alluding to the fact that he was there to sexually satisfy his daughter, so she didn't need a husband.[1]

## STRANGE GOINGS-ON

In the days leading up to the murders, Andreas told neighbours about some odd occurrences that had been unfolding at the farm. A Munich newspaper was discovered on the kitchen windowsill, which the family found peculiar because it was not a local newspaper. When Andreas questioned the postman, Joseph Mayer, about it, he denied that he had delivered the newspaper to anybody in the area. When Andreas looked out at the snow-covered farmland, he noticed footprints leading from the edge of the nearby dark forest to the farm, but none leading back. Was there a trespasser? Was someone watching the family? Kreszenz Rieger certainly thought so. While working at the farm, she was so convinced that somebody – or something – was lurking in the shadows of the forest that, just months before the murders, she packed her bags and fled, never to return. At around the same time, the house keys disappeared from Andreas' desk and somebody attempted to break into the engine yard.

The **postman** noticed that the letters he had delivered on Saturday were left untouched.

Viktoria sang in the **church choir** so her absence was particularly noticed.

Andreas also voiced concerns that livestock was missing and that somebody was creeping around in his attic. Over the course of several nights, he heard strange noises coming from above, but when he went to investigate, he found nothing. His neighbour urged him to go to the police but Andreas refused, saying, "I know how to defend myself."

While these incidents were cause for concern, nobody could have expected what happened next. From 1 April 1922, the entire Gruber family seemed to have vanished. Cäzilia did not appear at school that day – a Saturday – and the family didn't attend church on Sunday.

# 4 April 1922 / The bodies of the Gruber family are discovered.

Each of the six victims suffered **fatal blows** to the head.

Three neighbours decided to investigate. Discovering that all of the doors were locked, they broke into the barn adjoining the farmhouse. Daylight penetrating the murky barn illuminated a ghastly sight: the bludgeoned bodies of Andreas, his wife Cäzilia, Viktoria and her daughter Cäzilia, piled up among the hay. From the barn, the neighbours were able to enter the farmhouse, where they found the lifeless bodies of the maid, Maria, and little Josef.

## THE INVESTIGATION BEGINS

Kreszenz's replacement, Maria, was murdered on the very **first day** she started work at Hinterkaifeck farm.

The police concluded that the first four victims had been lured one by one to the barn and murdered before they could even cry out. The killer stacked their bodies one on top of the other and partially covered them with hay and an old door that had been dumped in the barn. He then went into the farmhouse, where he killed Josef, who was asleep in his cot, and Maria. He covered their bodies with clothing and sheets.

Each victim had been bludgeoned with a mattock – a pickaxe-like farming tool – on the face and head. The elder Cäzilia also showed signs of strangulation. While the majority died a quick, albeit vicious, death, the younger Cäzilia took several hours to die. The pathologist discovered tufts of her hair tangled in her fingers and in her hands. She had apparently pulled some of it out as she lay dying.

The pathologist estimated that the murders took place at around 9:30 p.m. on 31 March. Furthermore, the killer did not immediately flee the grisly scene – he remained at the farm for several days, feeding and milking livestock and helping himself to bread and ham from the pantry. Neighbours later claimed that they had seen smoke coming from the farmhouse chimney.

The **family dog** had been tied up in a barn but was unharmed.

## HINTERKAIFECK FARM

**A** Farm location

**B** Forest

**C** Maid's bedroom – Maria's body

**D** Children's bedroom – Josef's body

**E** Bodies of Andreas, Cäzilia senior, Viktoria and Cäzilia junior

**F** Kitchen

**G** Barn

**H** Footprints to the house

*Above:* Hinterkaifeck farm, some 251 metres (275 yds) from the outskirts of Gröbern.

26

Schrobenhausen police were called in to assist in the investigation, but after realising that they were in over their heads, the more experienced Munich force took over the case. Their initial theory was that the killer was a vagrant, motivated by the family's considerable wealth. However, a search of the farm indicated that gold coins and jewelry had been untouched, and no belongings or livestock were missing.

When police questioned local residents, the name Josef Bartl came to their attention. Bartl was a serial robber who had once escaped a mental asylum. In 1919, he had robbed the Alder family in the small village of Ebenhausen, about 13 miles (21 km) from Hinterkaifeck. Many speculated that only a madman like Josef would have remained at the crime scene, living alongside the bloody bodies of his victims for so many days. However, other than the most tenuous circumstantial evidence, nothing tied him to the crime.

## PAST LOVES

Mayor Lorenz Schlittenbauer, who had once wanted to marry Viktoria and had possibly fathered Josef, was a prime suspect throughout the investigation. He was one of the three neighbours who discovered the bodies and he lived the closest to Hinterkaifeck farm. He had clashed violently with Andreas over his relationship with Vicktoria, and had even reported them to the authorities for their incestuous relationship. According to the other neighbours on the scene, Schlittenbauer was also said to have been remarkably unfazed when the Grubers' bodies were discovered, despite the gruesome nature of what they found. Admittedly, this outwardly calm behaviour could be attributed to shock.

## 30 March 1931 / Lorenz Schlittenbauer is interrogated about the murders once more.

Lorenz Schlittenbauer was interrogated at the crime scene on 5 April 1922. At the time of the murders, he claimed he was a happily married man with no motive for killing the entire Gruber family. Nevertheless, even today, Schlittenbauer remains a favourite suspect among the townsfolk of Ingolstadt. Schlittenbauer's family still lives in the town and still has to endure the whispers and speculation that he was the killer, even though, as his son Alois pointed out, "there has never been an indictment."

One of the more outlandish suspects was Viktoria's ex-husband, Karl Gabriel, who had supposedly died in the trenches in 1914. His body was never actually retrieved, leading the Schrobenhausen chief of police, Ludwig Meixl, to suggest that perhaps Gabriel had not died at all. If he had survived, he could have travelled to Hinterkaifeck and committed the murders, perhaps in revenge for his wife's incestuous affair with her father. However, on 12 December 1923, Karl Gabriel's death was officially confirmed by the Central Prosecution Office for War Losses and War Graves, and he was officially ruled out as a suspect in the case.

## OTHER POSSIBILITIES

Another surprising suspect was the cruel and controlling head of the family, Andreas Gruber himself. Author Adolf Jakob Köppel argued in an article in the Munich newspaper *Abendzeitung* that the mattock used to kill the victims was handmade by Gruber himself and would have been difficult for an untrained person to wield with such deadly efficiency.[2] However, this theory fails to explain how Andreas could have inflicted such fatal injuries on himself.

# "THE DEVIL CAME TO HINTERKAIFECK – BUT HE WAS ALREADY THERE..."
ADOLF JAKOB KÖPPEL

Twenty years later, in 1941, an elderly neighbour, Kreszentia Mayer, made a deathbed confession to her priest, Anton Hauber. She stated that her brothers Adolf and Anton Gump were responsible for the Hinterkaifeck murders. She explained that her oldest brother, Adolf, had been in an intimate relationship with Viktoria and had been infuriated when he became aware of Viktoria and Andreas Gruber's incestuous relationship.

According to Kreszentia Mayer, Adolf and Anton had killed Viktoria and Andreas Gruber, and then dispatched everyone else living at the farm to ensure that there would be no witnesses to reveal their crime. However, it was not until 1952 that police decided to investigate the brothers' possible guilt. By this time, Adolf had been dead for eight years and Anton was an elderly pensioner who categorically denied any involvement in the murders. He was arrested but, after three weeks in custody, released without charge.

## A DARK LEGACY

The most recent questioning on the case took place in **1986**.

While the heads were in Munich, they were sent to a **clairvoyant** who claimed that two people had committed the murders.

The combination of the unexplained footprints in the snow leading from the forest to the farm, and the mysterious sounds apparently coming from the attic, paint a frightening picture of a sadistic intruder hiding in the house and waiting for his moment to strike. This picture continues to fascinate professional and amateur sleuths many decades after the slayings. However, the sheer lack of evidence, incomplete case records, and the deaths of potential witnesses and suspects means that it is doubtful the mystery of the Hinterkaifeck murders will ever be solved. During the chaos of World War II, a significant number of the police files were destroyed. In addition, all six of the victims' heads, which had been sent to the Pathology Institute of the University of Munich for analysis, also disappeared.

One year after the mass murders at Hinterkaifeck, a court order was given for the farmhouse and outbuildings to be demolished. A small marble monument near the original site, along with six graves for the family and their maid, is all that now remains to mark the horrors that unfolded all those years ago.

# THE IMPOSSIBLE MURDER

**Was this history-making case a "perfect crime" meticulously orchestrated by a ruthless mastermind? Or was the prime suspect just another innocent victim?**

The murder of Julia Wallace, bludgeoned to death in the parlour of her marital home in Liverpool, England on 20 January 1931 is widely regarded as one of the most baffling of all unsolved crimes. This classic "locked-room" murder mystery has fascinated crime writers such as Raymond Chandler and Dorothy L. Sayers, inspired the P. D. James novel *The Skull Beneath the Skin*, and also been the subject of a television drama, investigative documentaries, and numerous true crime books and articles in the press. The case also made British legal history: it was the first time that a murder conviction was overturned on appeal following a review of the evidence.

## THE HAPPY COUPLE

William Herbert Wallace and his wife, Julia, lived in a small, three-bedroom terrace on Wolverton Street in the poor district of Anfield, Liverpool. They had been married for 17 years. William had travelled widely as a young man, visiting both India and China. He was forced home by illness and met Julia a couple of years after his return to Britain. William was now an insurance agent with the Prudential

*Opposite page, main image:* Julia Wallace c.1900.
*Opposite page, clockwise from top:* Detective-sergeant Harry Bailey at the back door that would not – and then would – open; Julia Wallace's body in the parlour at 29 Wolverton Street; Richard Gordon Parry in a 1934 police mug shot; prime suspect William Wallace.

1 VICTIM | 3 KEY SUSPECTS

Assurance Company, while Julia was an amateur painter and pianist. In fact, both Julia and William were musically gifted, with William being an adept violin player. The couple would often play and sing duets together. Julia was exceptionally intelligent, having studied philosophy and dabbled in chemistry. According to William, their marriage was harmonious, and friends and neighbours would testify that there was nothing to indicate otherwise.

## MYSTERY CLIENT

On the evening of Monday, 19 January 1931, 52-year-old William Wallace arrived at the Liverpool Central Chess Club for a game. He was handed a message by club captain Samuel Beattie, who had taken a telephone call for Wallace. The caller had identified himself as "R. M. Qualtrough" and requested that Wallace should come to "25 Menlove Gardens East" the following evening at 7:30 p.m. to discuss an insurance deal. "I want to see him particularly," said the voice at the end of the line.[1] The caller said that he couldn't call back because it was his daughter's 21st birthday and he was therefore particularly busy. William took the note and placed it in his pocket, telling Beattie that he didn't know anybody by the name of "R. M. Qualtrough", but would visit him tomorrow nevertheless. Times were tough in Depression-era Britain and Wallace foresaw the possibility of some much-needed money.

The following evening, Wallace finished his day's work at the Prudential Assurance Company and returned home, where Julia had dinner waiting. When the couple finished eating, Wallace told her that he had a meeting with a man who could hopefully bring him more insurance business. As Wallace put on his coat, he added that he would be home as soon as possible.

**7:06 p.m. /** William Wallace boards the tram at Lodge Lane in order to keep his appointment with R. M. Qualtrough.

Julia claimed to be **much younger** than she was. She was actually 17 years older than William.

The **Liverpool Central Chess Club** met every Monday and Thursday at Cottle's city café at 24 North John Street.

William was known as an **enthusiastic** chess player rather than a good one, and only qualified for the second-class team.

The **milk boy** came to collect his money from Julia between 6:30 p.m. and 6:45 p.m.

Wallace set off for 25 Menlove Gardens East; he hadn't heard of the address before but knew the general area. During his tram journey, he chatted to the tram inspector, mentioning where he was going. Wallace got off the tram at what he assumed was the appropriate stop and went looking for the address. He found Menlove Gardens North, South and West, but no Menlove Gardens East. He then asked several people, including a couple of police officers on beat duty if they knew the street. They all gave the same answer: Menlove Gardens East did not exist.

His patience exhausted, Wallace gave up this infuriating wild goose chase and made his way back home, pondering who "R.M. Qualtrough" could be and why he had seen fit to send him to a non-existent address on a cold, dark winter's evening.

**25 Menlove Gardens West**
resident Katie Mather told Wallace she didn't know anyone named Qualtrough.

## THE MOVEMENTS OF WILLIAM WALLACE

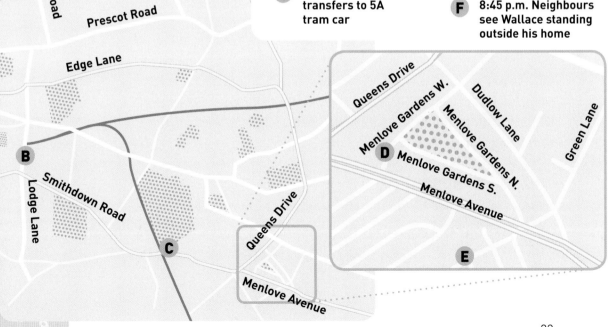

**A** Wallace leaves his house

**B** 7:06 p.m. Wallace boards tram

**C** 7:15 p.m. Wallace transfers to 5A tram car

**D** Katie Mather tells Wallace she does not know a Qualtrough

**E** 7:45 p.m. Wallace asks a policeman the time

**F** 8:45 p.m. Neighbours see Wallace standing outside his home

## THE BODY IN THE PARLOUR

Wallace arrived home – only to discover that he was unable to open either his front or back door. Both appeared to be locked from the inside. His next-door neighbours, John and Florence Johnston, saw him looking worried and asked him if he needed any help. He told them that he had been out for several hours and could not get into his home. However, while Mr and Mrs Johnston were present, he walked around to the back once again and this time, the door opened. "It opens now," he murmured to his neighbours. As he entered the house, a ghastly scene met his eyes. Julia was lying in front of the gas fire in the parlour. She had been bludgeoned to death with a heavy object, hit with such force that her skull had been cracked open. "They've finished her, look at her brains..." William commented, with a surprising lack of apparent emotion, to Mr and Mrs Johnston, who were standing behind him in the doorway.

Police soon arrived to assess the scene and make a search of the house and surrounding area. They noted that there was no sign of breaking and entering, leading them to believe that Julia herself must have admitted the killer into the house. A small sum of money had been stolen from an insurance money cashbox in the house but the police deduced that this was a ploy to give the impression that the murder was the result of a robbery gone wrong. The handling of the investigation left much to be desired; while examining the crime scene, officers wandered all over the house, and smudged fingerprints that could have belonged to the killer. Moreover, the pathologist neglected to take the temperature of Julia's body and therefore an accurate time of death was never determined.

## THE GUILTY HUSBAND?

What is known is that the murder was frenzied and brutal. Blood was splattered across the room, indicating that the killer would most likely have blood on his own clothes. In addition, a check of the house's sinks and drains revealed that they had not been used, indicating that the killer left without washing any blood from his clothing or body.

Anfield was in the grip of a spate of burglaries by the **"Anfield Housebreaker"**. Some thought he could have been the killer but no evidence tied him to the slaying.

Police found five people with the last name **Qualtrough** in the Liverpool area. All denied contacting the chess club.

Although there was no direct evidence against him, police soon began to question whether William had killed his wife and engineered the phony meeting with the mysterious "R. M. Qualtrough" to deflect suspicion from himself. They took the fact that William had asked various people for directions as a ploy to establish an alibi for the murder. It transpired that the phone call from "R.M. Qualtrough" had come from a telephone box just 366 metres (400 yds) from the Wallace household. However, Samuel Beattie, who had taken the phone call at the Liverpool Central Chess Club, was adamant that the voice on the other end of the line was not William's.

Investigators also questioned why William had claimed that the back door of his home was jammed but, as soon as other witnesses were present, miraculously opened. Investigators found a mackintosh beneath Julia's body. William didn't have a spot of blood on the suit he was wearing, so police speculated that he could have worn the mackintosh over his naked body as he carried out the murder to shield himself from blood spatter.

While investigators were building a case against William, the balance of evidence was beginning to tilt in his favour. Numerous witnesses placed William on the tram at around 7:06 p.m. that evening, while others claimed to have seen Julia alive at approximately 6:45 p.m. This time frame implied that William would only have had about 20 minutes to murder his wife, clean himself up, dispose of the murder weapon, hide the money that was missing from the cashbox *and* catch the tram.

**The milk boy** came to collect his money from Julia between 6:30 p.m. and 6:45 p.m.

## February 2, 1933 / William Herbert Wallace is arrested and charged with the murder of Julia Wallace.

William stood trial at Liverpool Assizes. "Few more brutal murders can ever have been committed – this elderly, lonely woman literally hacked to death for apparently no reason at all," declared the prosecuting counsel, Edward Hemmerde K.C. During the trial, William seemed detached and monotone, if not cold, while detailing the events around the horrible murder of a loved one. He took the stand and failed to impress the jury. Why? As an observer of the trial, crime writer

F. Tennyson Jesse wrote: "The jury did not like the man, or his manner which could have been either stoicism or callousness. They did not understand his lack of expression... and they knew it hid something. It could have hidden sorrow or guilt and they made their choice."

All the evidence against William was highly circumstantial and no motive was put forward. Nevertheless, after just an hour of deliberation by the jury, William Herbert Wallace was found guilty of his wife's murder and sentenced to die on the gallows.

The trial of William Wallace was extremely short, lasting just **four days**.

# "PEOPLE OF UNPLEASING PERSONALITY SHOULD BE ADVISED NEVER TO GO INTO THE WITNESS BOX."
CRIME WRITER F. TENNYSON JESSE

One month later, Wallace became the first man in Britain to have a conviction for murder dismissed on the grounds that it was not supported by the evidence. Wallace was a free man, but was still met with general suspicion. He moved to a bungalow on the River Mersey where, just two years later, he died. Some said that stress and a broken heart contributed to his sudden demise. He went to the grave protesting his innocence. Wallace was buried beside his wife.

## ALTERNATIVE SUSPECTS

So if William Herbert Wallace was not responsible for his wife's murder, then who killed her? In 1984, true crime writer Roger Wilkes speculated in his book *Wallace: The Final Verdict* that the real murderer of Julia Wallace was Richard Gordon Parry, a former work colleague of Wallace. Another former colleague told police that Wallace had reported Parry for wrongdoing, which led to Parry being fired. In his book, Wilkes claims that Parry wanted revenge on Wallace, so he lured Wallace from his home with the phone call and committed the murder while Wallace was out searching for the non-existent address. While researching the case, Wilkes found a new witness; a retired mechanic named John Parkes, who claimed that on the night of Julia Wallace's murder, he had hosed down a car for Parry. While cleaning the car's interior, he came across a bloodstained glove, which Parry quickly snatched away.[3]

John Gannon's book *The Killing of Julia Wallace* named another suspect in the murder: Joseph Caleb Marsden. Gannon theorised that Wallace knew that he did not have long to live and decided that he did not want to spend his final years with his hated wife. According to Gannon, Wallace hired Parry to make the bogus phone call in order to provide Wallace with an iron-clad alibi for the time of the murder.

However, Gannon contended that neither Wallace nor Parry committed the murder, but Marsden. Gannon asserted that Marsden was about to marry into a wealthy family, but Wallace had discovered that he was having a sexual relationship with Julia. This gave Wallace the opportunity to blackmail Marsden into killing his wife for him. During the initial investigation, however, Marsden's name cropped up as nothing more than an acquaintance of both Wallace and his wife.[4]

## AN UNSOLVABLE PUZZLE

Since 1931, the so-called "perfect murder" of Julia Wallace has been investigated and reinvestigated numerous times. Nevertheless, experts still have contradicting opinions on William Herbert Wallace's guilt. Many wild rumours circulated, from William having an affair with Julia's sister to Julia being overinsured and killed by William for the money. One of the most imaginative theories in the case is that William was a secret disciple of occultist Aleister Crowley with a drug addiction, who had numerous affairs behind his wife's back. However, no evidence has ever substantiated any of these speculations.

The murder of Julia Wallace continues to defy explanation. The crime novelist Raymond Chandler fittingly referred to the case as "the nonpareil of all murder mysteries... the impossible murder, because Wallace couldn't have done it and neither could anyone else".

# DEEP WATERS

**By an extraordinary twist of fate, a human arm expelled by a shark became the first link in a bizarre chain of events involving smuggling, blackmail and murder.**

It was a balmy spring afternoon on 17 April 1935. Bert Hobson and his son Ron were fishing from a 3.6-metre (12-ft) launch off Maroubra Point in Coogee, Sydney, Australia. Dissatisfied with their catch so far, they put out set lines baited with horse mackerel before returning home for the evening. The following morning, they returned to see if their set lines had caught anything profitable. They were surprised to discover a tiger shark measuring a mighty 4.42 metres (14 ft 6 in). The shark had been lured to the set line to feast on a smaller shark that had become tangled in it. The Hobsons managed to capture the tiger shark and then sold it to the Coogee Aquarium, which happened to be run by Bert's brother Charlie. The worldwide economic depression of the 1930s had hit Sydney hard, and Charlie Hobson hoped that this exciting addition would attract visitors willing to pay a bit extra to see the impressive shark fed twice a day.

## THE TATTOOED ARM

On the afternoon of 25 April, Anzac Day (a holiday honouring veterans), eight days after the shark had been caught, a grisly discovery surfaced

*Opposite page, main image:* The Coogee Aquarium, Sydney, where a recently captured tiger shark sparked a baffling murder mystery.
*Opposite page, left to right:* The victim, James Smith; key witness Reginald Holmes; Cored Joy, the seaside cottage rented by suspect Patrick Brady.

1 VICTIM | 1 DISMEMBERED ARM | 2 KEY SUSPECTS

in the shark's tank. Fortunately, only a few people were present when the aquarium's prize attraction started to thrash about, almost as if it was about to jump out of the pool. Moments later a human arm – clearly expelled by the shark – was spotted bobbing in the water. While Bert Hobson used a stick to keep this gruesome find close to the side of the tank, in case the huge shark tried to swallow it again, the police were immediately informed and rushed to the scene. To their surprise, the arm appeared to be in a fair state of preservation. Generally, the gastric juices of a shark would digest human flesh within days. However, the stress and shock of being captured and put on display may have slowed the shark's digestive processes. A piece of rope was tied around the wrist and, on the inside forearm, was a tattoo of two sparring boxers.

It was thought that the arm had actually been swallowed by the **smaller shark** that the tiger shark had eaten.

*Above:* A reconstruction of the distinctive boxers tattoo on the severed arm.
*Left:* The tiger shark in Coogee Aquarium

## A MISSING BROTHER

Gradually, theories as to whose arm it was started to build. Some wondered whether the arm had been discarded by a doctor or medical student, while others suggested, rather fancifully, that the arm could have belonged to a man who had committed suicide by plunging into the ocean with his arms tied. Due to decomposition, fingerprinting was no easy task. Medical examiners had to carefully remove skin from the fingers and then slip it over their own gloved digits to lift a print.

# 29 April 1935 / Edwin Smith contacts police to report that the arm belongs to his missing brother James.

Police received their first lead when a man named Edwin Smith recognised the description of the tattoo. Edwin's brother James had been missing since 7 April, after telling his wife that he was "going on a fishing trip with a companion". James was a 45-year-old, English-born criminal, police informant, and ex-boxer who lived in the Sydney suburb of Gladesville. Fingerprinting confirmed that the arm did indeed belong to him.

It was initially assumed that its discovery was simply evidence of another tragic shark attack, of which there had been three in recent months. However, further examination revealed a far more disturbing scenario. It was clear that the arm had not been bitten off by the shark after all – it had been severed with a knife. The focus of the investigation suddenly shifted to murder.

Thanks to Edwin Smith's information, the police at least knew who the arm belonged to; however, they were now faced with arguably the most bizarre case they had ever encountered. In a *Wagga Wagga Express* article, dated 15 June 1935, detectives freely admitted that they were facing a problem seemingly devised "by one of the cleverest killers in the history of Sydney's crime".

James Smith had been missing for more than **three weeks**.

## SHADY DEALS

James Smith had numerous connections with the criminal underworld and, while looking into his seedy acquaintances, investigators came across the name Reginald Holmes. To many who knew him, Holmes appeared to be a respectable, wealthy businessman and family man who ran a successful boat-building business on the shores of Lavender Bay. However, there was another, hidden side to Holmes' life. Behind the façade of normality, he was involved in various illegal activities, controlling lucrative smuggling and insurance fraud operations from his company, which was strategically situated on the shorefront. Enquiries revealed that Holmes had once hired Smith to collect cocaine, opium and other contraband dropped overboard by ships coming in from the east. Moreover, investigators discovered that the year before his disappearance, Smith had been using an overinsured yacht owned by Holmes when it mysteriously caught fire and sank. The duo had intended to cash in on the insurance money, but the company concerned became suspicious and refused to pay.

Investigators speculated that Smith was shot dead on the shore and his body then dumped in the ocean. They hoped that finding the spent cartridge from the bullet that killed him, as well as identifying the gun that fired it, might lead them to his killer.

The beaches from Cronulla to Coogee were painstakingly searched. The shark in the aquarium was also killed, gutted and examined. However, both of these attempts to find any clues as to how Smith met his end were in vain.

## HARBOR CHASE

Initially, Holmes strongly denied any involvement in the bizarre case. But shortly after police questioned him, they received reports of a "raving man" careening around the harbour in a speedboat with blood streaming down his face. After a lengthy police pursuit, the dazed man was captured and identified as Reginald Holmes. He had a wound on his head, and he claimed that somebody had shot at him. However, the police were skeptical of this story and concluded that Holmes had inflicted the gunshot wound on himself. Either Holmes was trying to cast himself as a victim in the case, or the graze on his head was a failed suicide attempt.

Interrogation of Holmes then led investigators to a convicted forger named Patrick Brady. Investigators discovered that Smith was last seen drinking and playing cards with Brady at the Hotel Cecil in Cronulla. They also found out that Brady had rented a small cottage called "Cored Joy" on Taloombi Street in Cronulla.

When the cottage was searched, a can of kerosene mixed with blood was found in the pantry. The owner of the cottage noticed that since

Patrick Brady had several **aliases**, including Mr Williams, Mr Anderson, and Mr Evans.

Brady had rented it, two rugs, two large mats, a mattress, a metal trunk, and a rope all appeared to be missing. Even more peculiar, the contents of the missing metal trunk had been placed inside a new, larger one that was found in its place. The owner also noted that the cottage had been scrupulously cleaned. Impressed by this accumulation of clues, the police questioned Patrick Brady and a few days later, they charged him with the murder of James Smith.

## 12 June 1935 / Reginald Holmes, the key witness in Patrick Brady's murder trial, is found shot dead in his car.

Reginald Holmes was scheduled to appear at the coroner's inquiry, as well as the much-anticipated trial of Brady. However, Holmes would not live long enough to give his testimony. In the early hours of the very morning of the coroner's enquiry, Holmes was found shot dead in his car on Hickson Road, Dawes Point, near Sydney Harbour Bridge. This desolate, run-down area was somewhere that law-abiding citizens tended to avoid. It was reputed to be a favourite meeting point for local smugglers – a place where money and contraband speedily changed hands.

On the night of Reginald Holmes' murder, a man fishing off Dawes Point claimed he heard **three shots** at around 9:00 or 10:00 p.m.

The passenger door of Holmes' Nash sedan was ajar and the position of his wounds indicated that he had been shot three times by someone sitting in the passenger seat. Moreover, there were no signs of a struggle, implying that Holmes had been murdered by somebody he knew well enough to allow into his car.

### MRS. HOLMES

Following Holmes' murder, his wife came forward to divulge what she knew, and in lieu of her murdered husband, became the key witness in the trial. She said that on 8 April, Patrick Brady had visited their home; his arms were cut and bloody, and he carried a knapsack that she recognised as belonging to Smith. A taxi driver would later corroborate her story, telling investigators that, on that same date, he had driven Brady from Cronulla to Holmes' home in North Sydney.

After Brady left, Holmes told his wife that Brady had murdered Smith, dismembered him, and "put it in a tin trunk, put it in a boat and tipped it overboard".[1]

# "HE HAD A HAND IN A POCKET AND WOULDN'T TAKE IT OUT... IT WAS CLEAR [HE] WAS FRIGHTENED."

A TAXI DRIVER TESTIFIES AT THE TRIAL OF PATRICK BRADY

A majority of the detectives in the Sydney homicide squad believed that Brady somehow forgot about Smith's telltale tattooed arm when packing the trunk with the rest of his dismembered remains. Realizing his mistake, he later disposed of it, whereupon it was swallowed by the shark. Others theorised that Brady had retained Smith's arm as evidence, in order to convince Holmes that the gruesome deed had been done, before disposing of it.

**48** witnesses were subpoenaed for the murder trial of Patrick Brady.

## REJECTED TESTIMONY

The Supreme Court ruled that an arm did not constitute a body, which was required for a murder conviction, and thus there was no way of knowing if James Smith was deceased or not. The judge also refused to accept Mrs. Holmes testimony, regarding it only as hearsay.

The notoriety of the Shark Arm case blighted Patrick Brady's life. He died in 1965, aged **71.**

# 12 September 1935 / Patrick Brady is formally acquitted of the murder of Reginald Holmes.

The generally accepted theory is that when the insurance company refused to pay out after the suspicious sinking of Holmes' yacht, Smith and Holmes fell out, and Smith threatened to expose Holmes as a criminal. James Smith's wife testified that she found an entry in her husband's black pocket book that Reginald Holmes had owed him £60 or £65 (£4,100 or £4,486 today). She said she could not be sure how the debt was incurred. However, it is possible that this was the amount Holmes owed Smith for the boat insurance scheme that went awry. In a bid to save his reputation, Holmes hired Brady to put Smith away for good, and Brady shot Smith dead in his rented cottage. When investigators later questioned Holmes, Brady believed that Holmes would not stand up to the pressure, so he silenced him.

An intriguing alternative theory about Holmes' death was put forward by Alex Castles in his 1995 book, *The Shark Arm Murders*. Castles speculated that the outwardly respectable Holmes could have taken out a contract on his own life in order to spare his family the public shame they would have suffered if he were to be convicted of the boat insurance fraud.[2]

Alex Castles also suggested another possible suspect for the murders of Smith and Holmes. Smith had been a police informant and had pointed the finger at a Sydney gangster named Eddie Weyman in a bank robbery. Weyman was also mixed up in the local drug trade, and it is possible that Weyman killed Smith and Holmes out of revenge, and to remove rivals in the drug trade.

## EXPOSING THE TRUTH

Whoever threw James Smith's dismembered arm to the sharks and silenced Reginald Holmes has never been brought to justice. Had the trial of Patrick Brady taken place in modern times the outcome could well have been very different.

In 1954, somebody attempted to kill James Smith's son, Raymond Smith, with a **car bomb**. Fortunately, no one was in the car when the bomb exploded.

In the past, murder convictions without a body were rare, but modern developments in forensic science have made it much more likely that a conviction can be obtained today. A famous example is the conviction of Richard Crafts, who murdered his wife in Connecticut in 1986 and disposed of her body using a wood chipper. DNA technology in criminal investigation would probably have resulted in Brady being found guilty, with or without the rest of Smith's body. As it was, it was a million-to-one chance that the murder of James Smith was ever brought to light, triggering a chain of events that even the most ingenious thriller writer would have difficulty conceiving.

# PANIC IN THE CITY

**Who was the Mad Butcher of Kingsbury Run? This serial killer led one of the US's premier detectives in a gruesome dance, and terrified the citizens of Cleveland for four bloody years.**

*"Floating down the river, chunk by chunk by chunk;*
*Arms and legs and torsos, hunk by hunk by hunk!"*[1]

If you're from Cleveland then there's a good chance that you have heard this 1930s ditty. The eerie lyrics refer to the Cleveland Torso Murderer. This shadowy individual was exceptionally brutal – decapitating, dismembering and sexually mutilating his victims, many of whom were still alive when he inflicted these gruesome acts upon them. The Butcher would then litter Kingsbury Run – a shantytown in a creek bed running from East 90th Street and Kinsman Road to the Cuyahoga River – with their discarded limbs, ready to be found by unsuspecting passersby.

This story unfolded on the calm shores of Euclid Beach in Bratenahl, Ohio, on 5 September 1934. Frank Legassle was gathering wood when he made a grisly discovery that he initially mistook for a log. Bobbing along with the flow of the murky water was the decomposed torso of a woman; her head, arms and legs below the

*Opposite page, main image:* The burning of Kingsbury Run; letter supposedly from the killer.
*Opposite page, clockwise from top:* Postcard sent to Eliot Ness by Dr Francis Sweeney; Safety Director Eliot Ness; a drawing of a suspect; Frank Dolezal after confessing to the murders; Coroner Samuel Gerber examines bones said to be of the 11th and 12th victims.

**13 VICTIMS | 2 KEY SUSPECTS**

lice Matowitz,

ou can rest
nter. I felt
I shall soon

hat did thei
se twisted bo
No one missed
the feeling
Right now I h
me mad and

the he
tween estern and
odies I do. it

minus features is buried in a gu
Crenshaw. I feel it is
's will not to let them suffe

MSS3699
THOSE GLENWOOD
NILLS MENTAL DEFECTIV
IS

POST CARD

ELIOT. (ESOPHOGOTIC) NESS

UNION-COMMERCE
BUILDING.
CLEVELAND
OH.O.

WALT SWAN
TO SHOWER TIE
BUTTON OR CUT

UNITED
STATES

2 CENTS 2

knee were missing. The body had been treated with some kind of chemical preservative in an attempt to delay decomposition. Although never officially confirmed, she is generally accepted as the first victim of the Cleveland Torso Murderer. It would not be until the following year that Cleveland police realised that this macabre find was no isolated incident. There was a serial killer in their midst.

The identity of the first victim was never discovered, and she was dubbed **"The Lady of the Lake"**.

## TERRIBLE DISCOVERIES

The date was 23 September 1935, and Cleveland was swarming with worshippers gathering for the National Eucharistic Congress. While playing softball in a ravine in Kingsbury Run, just at the foot of Jackass Hill, two boys stumbled across the bodies of two men who had been decapitated and emasculated. One was identified via fingerprints as Edward Andrassy, 28, a petty criminal from Cleveland's West Side. He had rope burns around his wrists, presumably from being bound by his killer. The other man, who was stocky and middle-aged, was never identified but appeared to have been killed several weeks before Andrassy. Disturbingly, the professional-looking decapitations were not carried out postmortem, but were the cause of death for both men.

A 1937 *St. Louis Post-Dispatch* article described Edward Andrassy as **"an undesirable"**.

# 1934 / Safety Director Eliot Ness is transferred to Cleveland.

The famed Prohibition agent Eliot Ness was currently Cleveland's Safety Director, with a remit to clean up the city's notorious organised crime networks. However, a very different kind of criminal was now in Cleveland and Ness was determined to catch him.

Four months later, a barking dog drew attention to two half-bushel baskets covered with burlap bags discarded behind Hart Manufacturing, just off East 20th Street. Stuffed inside the baskets were the lower half of a female torso, two thighs, a right arm and a hand. The rest of her remains – apart from her head – were discovered the following week in a vacant lot a couple of blocks away on Orange Avenue. The cause of death was decapitation; her head had

Eliot Ness had successfully led an operation against **Al Capone** and other Chicago mobsters.

been severed between the third and fourth cervical vertebrae with one swift stroke. Fingerprints enabled investigators to identify the body as Florence Polillo, a 42-year-old barmaid and prostitute from the Kingsbury Run area. This was the last of the Butcher's 13 victims that investigators would successfully identify.

Victim number five was discovered in June 1936. This time, two boys were skipping school when they happened upon a pair of trousers rolled into a ball lying near train tracks in Kingsbury Run. Hoping to find money in the pockets, they prodded the object with a fishing rod.[2]

# "WE TOOK A FISHING POLE AND POKED THE BUNDLE AND OUT POPS A HEAD."

THE BOY WHO FOUND THE FIFTH VICTIM

Investigators found a nude male body around 274 metres (300 yds) away, in front of the Nickel Plate Road police building. Much like his male predecessors, the victim had been emasculated and decapitated. Investigators anticipated that this victim would be easy to identify owing to the fact that he had a number of tattoos, including a dove on his arm with the names "Helen-Paul" inscribed above it. However, despite these distinctive markings and a death mask being placed on display at the subsequent Great Lakes Exposition, his identity was never discovered.

## THE KILLINGS CONTINUE

Between 1925 and 1940, several bodies eerily similar to those of the Cleveland victims were found in an area known as **"Murder Swamp"** in New Castle, Pennsylvania.

A pattern was beginning to emerge: decapitation, dismemberment and sexual mutilation, all skillfully performed. As investigators sought the brutal killer, the bodies continued to pile up. In mid-July, another victim was found in a valley similar to Kingsbury Run on the west side of the city. He had been decapitated and emasculated; the head was found 3 metres (10 ft) away alongside a bundle of bloody clothing.

The substantial amount of blood on the ground indicated that, unlike previous victims, this man had been killed on the spot. In September, remains of a seventh victim were discovered in a stagnant creek in Kingsbury Run. Near his body was a bloodstained shirt wrapped in a newspaper. The creek was dragged by divers until the lower halves of his legs were found. He, too, had been emasculated; his head was never recovered.

## GRUESOME DISCOVERIES

The year 1937 brought a spate of new bodies. On 23 February, the upper part of a young woman's torso was found on Lake Erie's rocky eastern shore. Unlike those before her, she had been decapitated postmortem. The lower half of her torso washed ashore three months later. Bones and a skull were all that remained of victim number nine, who was found on 6 June. They were unearthed beneath the Lorain-Carnegie Bridge, less than a mile from Kingsbury Run. Analysis of the bones revealed that they were those of an African-American woman who had been dead about a year. As the news spread throughout the city, a man claimed that the remains were those of his mother, Rose Wallace, who had disappeared 10 months earlier. However, this was never officially confirmed.

Investigators did not have to wait long for yet another body to appear. On July 6, the lower half of a man's torso was found floating in the Cuyahoga River. A burlap sack containing his upper torso was retrieved later. This victim had been sliced open, gutted and had his heart ripped out.

There was a respite until April of the following year, when a young labourer saw something floating near a sewer outlet flowing into the Cuyahoga River. At first glance, he thought it was a dead fish, but on closer inspection, he realised it was the lower half of a woman's leg. In the coming weeks, a lung, a knot of intestines and a thigh would be found in the river, along with two burlap sacks, one of which contained two halves of a torso. Frustratingly, the second sack – which may have contained the head – sank without a trace.

Lake Erie

St. Clair Ave.

Superior Ave.

Euclid Ave.

Woodland Ave.

Kinsman Rd

Detroit Ave.

E 49th St

Broadway Ave.

Harvard Ave.

## LIST OF VICTIMS

**A**    5 September 1934: Victim 1 (unknown woman, Lady of the Lake)

**B**    23 September 1935: Victim 2 (Edward Andrassy),
victim 3 (unknown man)

**C**    26 January 1936: Victim 4 (Florence Polillo)

**D**    5 June 1936: Victim 5 (unknown man)

**E**    22 July 1936: Victim 6 (unknown man)

**F**    10 September 1936: Victim 7 (unknown man)

**G**    23 February 1937: Victim 8 (unknown woman)

**H**    6 June 1937: Victim 9 (possibly Rose Wallace)

**I**    6 July 1937: Victim 10 (unknown man)

**J**    8 April 1938: Victim 11 (unknown woman)

**K**    6 August 1938: Victim 12 (unknown woman),
victim 13 (unknown man)

***Above:*** Weapons
used by the killer.

## NESS TAKES ACTION

Despite Eliot Ness and the Cleveland police's best efforts, they came no closer to catching the Mad Butcher of Kingsbury Run. They followed a profusion of leads, but every tip and search proved fruitless.

# 16 August 1938 / The bodies of the final two victims – a man and a woman – are discovered.

The final two victims were found on a landfill at East 9th and Lakeside. A female torso was wrapped in a man's blazer and then wrapped again in an old quilt. A nearby box containing the legs, arms and head was wrapped in brown butcher's paper. As investigators trudged among the garbage, they came across the remains of a male body in a more advanced state of decomposition than the woman found nearby. His head was found in a can. The landfill was in full view of Eliot Ness' office window, almost as if the killer was taunting the director.

Two days later, Ness raided the shantytown of Kingsbury Run, demanding that it be set alight and burned to the ground. Many residents left homeless were rounded up and arrested, as Ness presumed that the killer lived a transient lifestyle like his victims – without any evidence to back up this theory. According to him, the arrests were for the peoples' own protection, and also to collect fingerprints, making potential future victims easier to identify. At a time when unemployment and homelessness were rife, Ness was highly criticised for these extreme tactics. Nevertheless, following the destruction of Kingsbury Run, the killings finally stopped.

## WHO IS THE BUTCHER?

The Cleveland Torso Murderer's skill with a knife led to speculation that he must have extensive knowledge of human anatomy. Coroner Dr Samuel Gerber posited that the killer could be "a doctor, medical student, male nurse, an orderly, a butcher, hunter, or veterinary surgeon".[3] An article in the *Cleveland News* in 1936 described the killer as someone who "kills for the thrill of killing. He kills to satisfy a

In **1950**, 41-year-old Robert Robertson was found partially decapitated in Cleveland. Some theorised that he was another victim of the Cleveland Torso Murderer.

The police sent out advertisements in **44 languages,** encouraging people to report any discovery of large quantities of blood.

bestial, sadistic lust for blood. He kills to prove himself strong. He kills to feed his sex-perverted brain, the sight of a beheaded human. He must kill for decapitation is his drug, to be taken in closer-spaced doses". Investigators trawled through the city in search of the killer's "workshop".

# "YES, HE WILL KILL AGAIN. HE IS OF COURSE INSANE."
*CLEVELAND NEWS*, 1936

Despite the large number of people interviewed in connection with the case, the investigation came up with just one main suspect. In August 1939 the police arrested Frank Dolezal, a 52-year-old Slavic immigrant bricklayer who frequented the same downtown bar as the victims Polillo and Andrassy. A thorough search of his apartment turned up stains that investigators claimed were human blood, findings that seemed to clinch the case. Dolezal was questioned unrelentingly for two days, at the end of which he supposedly confessed to the murders.

However, other than circumstantial evidence, there was little to tie Dolezal to the slayings, and it did not take long for the case against him to start unravelling. There were also several discrepancies in Dolezal's so-called confession; he offered to direct investigators to the missing body parts, but led them on a fruitless search; in addition, the supposedly incriminating bloodstains found in his bathroom turned out to be from an animal. Dolezal then recanted his confession, claiming that the police had beaten it out of him. Before being brought to trial, the unfortunate Dolezal was found hanging dead in his cell.

The ensuing autopsy revealed bruises and six broken ribs, all of which were inflicted while in the custody of Sheriff Martin O'Donnell. Today, it is generally believed that Frank Dolezal was innocent of the Cleveland Torso Murders.

## THE SECRET SUSPECT

In 1938, Eliot Ness had another suspect who was never publicly identified. During Ness' grueling interrogation, this suspect was locked in a hotel room for two weeks – a clear violation of civil liberties. In his book *In the Wake of the Butcher,* James Badal named this "secret suspect" as Dr Francis Sweeney, a Cleveland physician and veteran of World War I. During his time in the army, Sweeney served as part of a medical unit that conducted work – including amputations – on the battlefield.

In 1934, a vagrant named Emil Fronek told police that he had escaped from a doctor who he believed to be the Cleveland killer. He recounted that a man "who looked like a doctor" offered him a meal at his home. He agreed and followed the man to a house in Kingsbury Run. Once inside, the doctor brought out "the finest handout I was ever offered". However, after scoffing the meal, Fronek became nauseated and fearful. When the man went into the kitchen – allegedly to get a whiskey – Fronek staggered outside and hid. He relayed his story to another vagrant, who also said that he "almost got cut up in that house, too". Unfortunately, Fronek was later unable to identify the house in Kingsbury Run where these events supposedly took place.

## DRUNK AND ABUSIVE

Francis Sweeney had lived a turbulent life; he was in and out of the probate court system and was an alcoholic. In fact, it was said that when Sweeney was apprehended by Ness, it took him two days to sober up enough to be able to cooperate. In 1934, Sweeney's wife divorced him on the grounds that he had become increasingly abusive and violent towards both her and their children. She said that he would disappear for days and hallucinate while under the influence of alcohol, causing her to fear for her safety and her husband's sanity. Nine days after the final victim was discovered, Sweeney committed himself to the Soldiers and Sailors Home in Sandusky, Ohio, where he was eventually diagnosed with schizophrenia. In the mid-1950s, Eliot Ness received several taunting postcards, supposedly from Sweeney.

It was later suggested that there could have been **multiple killers**, and that a lack of DNA testing and experience in handling such a case led investigators to attribute the slayings to one person.

In 2003, there was an attempt to retrieve DNA from the postage stamps on the letters, which were in possession of the Western Reserve Historical Society. Unfortunately, it was decided that this would cause too much irreparable damage to the items, and the DNA test was never carried out.

In 1939, Cleveland police had also received a letter which was reportedly from the Cleveland Torso Murderer. It read:

**Chief of Police Matowitz:**

**You can rest easy now, as I have come to sunny California for the winter. I felt bad operating on those people, but science must advance. I shall astound the medical profession, a man with only a D.C.**

**What did their lives mean in comparison to hundreds of sick and disease-twisted bodies? Just laboratory guinea pigs found on any public street. No one missed them when I failed. My last case was successful. I now know the feeling of Pasteur, Thoreau and other pioneers.**
**Right now I have a volunteer who will absolutely prove my theory. They call me mad and a butcher, but the truth will out.**

**I have failed but once here. The body has not been found and never will be, but the head, minus the features, is buried on Century Boulevard, between Western and Crenshaw. I feel it is my duty to dispose of the bodies as I do. It is God's will not to let them suffer.**
**X**

## LEGEND OF A KILLER

The Cleveland Torso Murders caused widespread panic among the city's rapidly growing population. Despite the frantic search for the killer, his identity remains a mystery – as does the identity of most of his unfortunate victims. The Torso Murders is still the most gruesome and notorious crime spree in the city's history. Today, Haunted Cleveland Ghost Tours even offer a "Torso Murder Tour", in which they tour the landmark sites of the murders and retrace the steps of the Mad Butcher of Kingsbury Run.

# SCANDAL IN SHANGRI-LA

**While most Britons were suffering the perils and privations of World War II, far away in Africa, a few wealthy aristocrats were living the high life. Until murder shattered their exotic idyll...**

The murder of Josslyn Hay, 22nd Earl of Erroll, Baron of Kilmarnock and High Constable of Scotland, scandalised wartime Britain by exposing the decadent habits of a group of wealthy expatriates in colonial Kenya. Speculation was also rife as to the murderer's possible motive. Was it a crime of passion prompted by Hay's notorious womanizing, or could his death have been a political assassination provoked by his fascist connections?

Hay was part of a small group of privileged white Britons sitting out the war by living a life of hedonism and luxury in Kenya. The group was known as the Happy Valley set, and the White Highlands of Kenya was their playground. The Happy Valley set became infamous for their debauched lifestyles; their sexual promiscuity, excessive drinking and drug use and continuous partying shocked the small community of settlers who were striving to create farmland from the African bush.

## WILD PARTIES

Hay first arrived in Kenya in 1924 with his wife, Lady Idina Sackville, with whom he had eloped while she was still married to her first

*Opposite page, main image:* The region of Kenya that was known as Happy Valley
*Opposite page, clockwise from left:* Lady Idina Gordon and her fiancé the Hon. Josslyn Hay, later Earl of Erroll, in 1923; Diana Caldwell; Hay in evening dress; Molly Ramsay-Hill on the day of her wedding to Hay; prime suspect Sir Jock Delves Broughton.

The TLER

POSTAGE
Inland, 2d.; Canada and New-
foundland, 1½d.; Foreign, 4½d.

Price
One Shilling

59
. 1923

**1 VICTIM | 2 KEY SUSPECTS**

LADY IDINA GORDON AND

A snapshot recently taken at a well-known Italian
sister, and the Hon. Josslyn Hay is a son of Lord
engagement of Lady Idina Gordon and Mr. Jo

husband. Hay barely pretended to be faithful, but Idina reportedly did not mind the numerous love affairs her husband was having behind her back. "Idina was only happy... if all her guests had swapped partners, wives or husbands by nightfall," wrote James Fox in his celebrated book on the Happy Valley case, *White Mischief*.[1] In fact, the couple's dinner parties at their ranch house, Clouds, were the talk of the area. A regular event at these gaudy soirées was the "sheet game", in which nude men lined up behind a sheet. The female guests then attempted to identify them just by their lower regions.

In 1928, the couple divorced amid rows over financial issues. Hay moved in with Edith Maude "Molly" Ramsay-Hill, a married woman some years Hay's senior. When Ramsay-Hill's husband was made privy to the affair, he confronted the couple and chased Hay with a rhino whip. Molly was soon divorced, and she and Hay wed in 1930.

After leaving her husband, Molly bankrolled both her and her younger husband. They lived in Oserian, a flashy, Moroccan-style home on the shores of Lake Naivasha, Kenya. Hay's chiselled looks, arrogant air and quick wit made him irresistibly attractive to the clique of bored, upper-class settlers' wives. A serial philanderer and gambler, his speciality was seducing rich married women. Meanwhile, Molly Ramsay-Hill so immersed herself in the alcohol and drug-fuelled "Happy Valley" lifestyle that she died of overindulgence in 1939.

## INSTANT ATTRACTION

The following year, Hay encountered Lady Diana Delves Broughton, a voluptuous 26-year-old with deep blue eyes and wispy blonde locks. Many women in the Happy Valley set envied her beauty and instant sex appeal. Lady Diana had recently married the much older Sir Jock Delves Broughton, 11th Baronet DL and the largest landowner in Kenya. Recently divorced, Sir Jock had decided to take his young wife to Kenya to escape his mounting debts, as well as to get away from wartime Britain.

The attraction between the rakish aristocrat Hay and Lady Diana was instant. They soon embarked upon a passionate and highly visible

James Fox's book was adapted into a 1987 film, also called **White Mischief**, starring Charles Dance as Hay, Greta Scacchi as Lady Diana and Joss Ackland as Sir Jock.

Hay's **shady reputation** dated back to his youth. In 1916, he was expelled from Eton for undisclosed reasons.

Shortly before Sir Jock divorced his first wife in 1939, he had been suspected of an **insurance fraud** over the theft of some paintings and jewellery.

**Lady Diana** was 30 years younger than her husband.

affair, which Sir Jock was said to be very nonchalant about. When he and Diana married, they had reportedly made a pact that they would "set each other free" should either one of them fall in love with somebody else. Sir Jock later claimed that he took a "philosophical" view of his beautiful young wife's affair with his friend and resolved to step back.[2]

As if to demonstrate that he bore the couple no ill will, on 23 January 1941, Sir Jock invited Lady Diana and Hay to a dinner party at the exclusive Muthaiga Club – a frequent haunt of the Happy Valley set – along with several other friends. During this lavish event, Sir Jock, though drinking heavily, played the perfect part of a graceful loser. He even toasted the new couple with champagne and wished them "every happiness".[3] Within hours, Hay would be dead.

## COVERED TRACKS

As the dinner party reached its drunken conclusion, Hay and Lady Diana decided to continue celebrating and went out dancing. At around 2:15 a.m., Hay dropped off Lady Diana at the home she shared with Sir Jock and climbed back into his Buick to drive the short distance to his own house. Scarcely an hour later, two dairy workers discovered his body. His car's headlights were still blazing.

# 24 January 1941 / Hay is found shot dead in his car at the Karen Road junction on the Nairobi-Ngong road.

Hay's body was in a kneeling position in the front passenger footwell; a bullet had entered his head just behind the right ear. Powder marks on the side of his face indicated that he had been shot at close range. In the car, police found a cigarette butt soaked in blood. In what remains arguably one of the most bungled police inspections in criminal history, Hay's body was removed before being carefully examined, and police trampled all over another set of tyre tracks that could have had a bearing on the case. Hay's Buick was even given a thorough wash before the decision was made to dust it for fingerprints.

The murder of Josslyn Hay, the 22nd Earl of Erroll. marked open season on his reputation, and stories of his hedonistic lifestyle flashed across British newspapers alongside news of the nightly raids by German bombers. He quickly became a symbol of debauched aristocracy and, eager for distraction from the Blitz, the nation reveled in his downfall. Before long, his affair with Lady Diana became common knowledge, and Sir Jock was named the prime suspect in the murder. He was duly arrested on 10 March and charged with Hay's murder. Sir Jock denied any involvement in the crime, citing the fact that he had invited Hay and Lady Diana to his dinner party the evening before the murder as evidence that he was not jealous or angry about the breakdown of his marriage.

# 26 May 1941 / The trial of Sir Jock Delves Broughton for the murder of Josslyn Hay, 22nd Earl of Erroll, begins.

During the subsequent trial, Lady Carberry, a close friend of the Broughtons, testified that, despite his protestations, Sir Jock appeared unhappy during the dinner party. He told her that he planned to give his wife his estate or make her an allowance. He also announced that he had been "extraordinarily lonely" during his short marriage.[4] Lady Carberry added that, after the death of Hay, on one occasion she and Sir Jock had lunch, during which he broke down and wept.

Lady Diana and Sir Jock were married for just **two months.**

### THE CASE COLLAPSES

So far, the evidence against Sir Jock was little more than supposition. The prosecution claimed that the bloodstained cigarette butt found in Hay's car constituted evidence that Sir Jock was the murderer, on the slender basis that Hay did not smoke, but Sir Jock was known to smoke two brands of cigarettes.

Searching for hard facts, the prosecution pinned its hopes on showing that the single bullet that killed Hay came from a .32 Colt found in Sir Jock's home. When a ballistics expert testified that the bullet that killed Hay could not have come from a Colt – any Colt – the absence of a murder weapon destroyed the prosecution's case. After just three hours deliberation, Sir Jock was acquitted. A contributing factor to this verdict may have been the fact that the foreman of the jury was Sir Jock's barber.

Far from being welcomed back after his ordeal, Sir Jock was shunned by his former Happy Valley friends. Lady Diana, apparently recovering quickly from the shock of Hay's murder, immediately left Sir Jock for Gilbert Colvile, a millionaire cattle rancher who lived nearby. Nursing a back injury, Sir Jock returned home to England alone and stayed in the Adelphi Hotel in Liverpool.

## 5 December 1942 / Sir Jock Delves Broughton commits suicide with a morphine overdose.

Lady Diana and Gilbert Colvile **divorced** amicably in 1955 and she married Lord Tom Delamere. She died, aged 76, on 3 September 1987.

Sir Jock **killed himself** just days after arriving in England.

To many observers, Sir Jock's suicide was tantamount to an admission of guilt. A month after Sir Jock's death, Lady Diana married the eminently respectable Gilbert Colvile.

In her 2003 book *Elspeth Huxley: a Biography*, C. S. Nicholls, an authority on colonial Kenya, named Sir Jock as the murderer. By her account, Sir Jock lay in wait for Hay when he drove Lady Diana home. He got in Hay's car, shot him and then drove to the crossroads. For a large sum of money, Sir Jock had arranged for an acquaintance, Dr Athan Philip, to meet him there and drive him back to his house.

### POLITICAL MOTIVES

The theory that Hay may have been killed by a jealous husband was one thing, but when Sir Jock was acquitted, speculation arose that there could have been a political motive for the murder. Could Hay have been assassinated by a British agent because he was a fascist sympathiser, suspected of collaborating with the Germans? Hay had actually joined the British Union of Fascists for a year in 1934; there were even rumors that he was involved in a renegade group that included the Duke of Windsor and Rudolf Hess.[5] An investigation by *The Sunday Times* speculated that Hay had abused his position as

The British Union of Fascists, led by **Oswald Mosley,** was banned in 1940 by the British government following the outbreak of World War II.

second-in-command of the Kenyan armed forces by selling secrets to Mussolini's forces in Italian East Africa. It was well known that British military plans had been leaked to the Italian army headquarters in Addis Ababa. Could Hay have been responsible? Giving more weight to this theory, several close associates of Lady Diana alleged that Hay was lined up to become the Governor of Kenya in the event of a successful Italian invasion.

## A LOVER'S REVENGE

Other commentators have suggested the possibility that a scorned lover did the deed. There are even some who believed that Hay was killed by Lady Diana when he refused to marry her. However, as their passionate romance was still in its first flush, and she was apparently at home in bed at the time of his death, this was thought unlikely.

In 2010, a fresh suspect was brought to light when Paul Spicer began researching the American heiress Countess Alice de Janzé, who had been a close friend of his mother and a leading member of the Happy Valley set.

In his book, *The Temptress: The Scandalous Life of Alice, Countess de Janzé*, Spicer related that Alice de Janzé had an on-off relationship with Hay over the course of several years. Coincidentally, she had experience with a gun, having shot her lover, the English nobleman and playboy Raymund de Trafford, and then herself at a Paris railway station in 1927. Both fortunately survived, and Alice de Janzé was dubbed "the fastest gun in the Gare du Nord".

Alice de Janzé was fined just **100 francs** (about $18 in US dollars) by the French court for shooting her lover and herself.

## THE FEMME FATALE

Alice de Janzé only received a six-month suspended sentence for shooting Raymund de Trafford and herself. The French court viewed the crime leniently as a "crime of passion". Spicer claimed that de Janzé had an issue with rejection and suggested that, incensed by Hay's budding relationship with the much younger Lady Diana Broughton, she could have arranged to meet Hay at the crossroads and shot him. "She had the motive and she certainly had the nerve.

**Left:** The tempestuous American heiress Countess Alice de Janzé confers with her barrister during her trial for shooting her lover and herself at the Gare du Nord, Paris,1927.

# "SHE HAD SHOT A MAN BEFORE."
AUTHOR PAUL SPICER, CONCERNING ALICE DE JANZÉ

She would not fear carrying out that act. She was consumed with jealousy." Soon after the murder, Alice de Janzé visited the mortuary where Hay's body lay and kissed him on the lips, reportedly exclaiming, "Now you are mine forever."

Alice de Janzé had dabbled in the occult and may have hoped to be reunited with her former lover in some form of afterlife. In any event, she never got over his death and committed suicide in September 1941. Spicer claimed that she left a note for the police in which she confessed to the murder. However, the contents of this letter have never been revealed.[6]

The glare of publicity surrounding the murder of Hay marked the beginning of the end for Kenya's colonial expat elite, but the question of who pulled the fateful trigger that dark night, and why, continues to cast its lurid, glamorous spell.

Alice de Janzé committed **suicide** just seven months after Hay's murder.

# THE SKELETON IN THE WOOD

**Was she a German spy, the victim of a black magic ritual, or an unfortunate vagrant? Who "Bella" really was is just one of this murder mystery's unanswered riddles.**

More than 75 years have passed since a woman's skeleton was found stuffed inside a wych elm in a park in Worcestershire during World War II. Following this grim discovery, cryptic graffiti asking the question "Who put Bella in the wych elm?" started to appear around the district. Bizarre theories of German spies and witchcraft rituals keep this local legend alive, and the strange and sinister tale of "Bella" still captivates armchair detectives today. Despite a lengthy police investigation and a plethora of plausible – and not so plausible – theories, the identities of the woman nicknamed "Bella", and that of her killer, remain a mystery.

## DOWN IN THE WOODS

The story of the case begins in fittingly dramatic fashion. As dusk was falling on 18 April 1943, four teenage boys were cautiously trudging through Hagley Woods. This stretch of woodland was situated on the grounds of the impressive Hagley Hall estate, which belonged to Lord Cobham. The four boys – Bob Hart, Tom Willetts, Fred Payne and Bob Farmer – were trespassing. Braving the dangers of getting caught by

*Opposite page, clockwise from top:* An artist's impression of "Bella" based on a police sketch; telltale graffiti on an obelisk on Wychbury Hill; the human skull that was found inside the wych elm in Hagley Wood; the German singer and actress Clara Bauerle, once suspected of being the mysterious "Bella".

WHO PUT
BELLA
IN THE
WITCH ELM

an angry gamekeeper, they were looking for some excitement to take their minds off the nightly German Luftwaffe's bombing raids, which were wreaking havoc in Birmingham, their hometown. They had their dogs with them and were hoping to supplement their families' meagre meat ration with a poached rabbit or two.

After a while, Bob Farmer spotted a wych elm – named for its strange appearance – and decided to climb it, hoping to find a bird's nest. He clambered up and peeked down into the hollow trunk. A glimmer of white convinced him that he had hit the jackpot. However, the object lodged in the middle of the tree was not a bird's nest; Bob pulled it out – and found himself staring at a skull, whose empty eye sockets seemed to stare right back at him. At first he thought that the skull was that of an animal, until he noticed clumps of what looked like human hair clinging to it, and crooked teeth protruding from its mouth. The boys fled the woods, promising each other never to tell a soul about what they had found, for fear of getting into trouble.

## THE WOMAN IN THE TREE

Despite the promise they had made, the seriousness of their find weighed heavily on 17-year-old Tom Willetts. Shortly after he returned home, he told his parents about what he and his friends had found in Hagley Woods and they alerted the police.

The area was soon cordoned off. Inside the ominous-looking tree, they found a woman's skeleton. Disturbingly, her hand was missing; the bones were discovered scattered around the tree. A cheap, imitation-gold ring and size 5-and-a-half crepe-soled shoes, were also found a short distance away. Scraps of poor-quality clothing hung from the bones, and a piece of taffeta fabric was stuffed inside the mouth of the skull, indicating that the victim had been suffocated. The medical examiner, Professor James Webster, concluded that the woman was around 35 years old, had irregular teeth in her upper jaw, had light brown hair, and was just 1.52 metres (5 ft) tall. He also determined that the woman had given birth to one child in her lifetime, and estimated that she had been dead for around 18 months.

In July 1941, a businessman and a schoolteacher had both reported hearing a **woman's scream** coming from Hagley Woods. Police searched the area but found nothing.

## October 1941 / The estimated time of death for the woman's skeleton discovered in the wych elm.

Professor Webster's findings made him certain that the death of this unknown woman was murder, stating: "I cannot imagine a woman accidentally slipping in there, neither do I think it reasonable for a woman to crawl into that place to commit suicide." He also concluded that the woman had been placed inside the hollow trunk before rigor mortis – the stiffening of the muscles following death – had set in; otherwise the body would have been too stiff to fit inside the narrow tree trunk. Professor Webster also maintained that the victim would most likely have been killed close to the spot where she was found; otherwise the killer would not have been able to transport her body to the tree before rigor mortis set in.

# "IT WAS AN EXCELLENT PLACE FOR THE CONCEALMENT OF A MURDER AND I THINK IT INDICATES LOCAL KNOWLEDGE."
MEDICAL EXAMINER PROF. JAMES WEBSTER

The police checked more than **3,000** missing persons files.

Following the discovery in the wych elm, Worcestershire police contacted every dentist in the area, hoping that one of them would recognise the woman's distinctive protruding teeth. They also trawled through piles of missing persons reports to see if any of them matched the description of the deceased. Neither line of enquiry turned up any leads. The investigation then turned towards the personal effects found at the scene. The crepe-soled shoes were traced to the Waterfoot Company, Lancashire, and investigators were able to find the owners of all but six pairs, which had been sold from a market stall in Dudley, a town roughly 18 km (11 miles) from Birmingham.

*Above:* The obelisk on Wychbury Hill, Hagley, Worcestershire, featuring the enigmatic graffiti.

## POLICE SKETCH

**A** Mock wedding ring

**B** Stripped knitted cardigan

**C** Cloth skirt with zip

**D** Blue, crepe-soled shoes

**E** Light blue belt

## MYSTERIOUS MESSAGES

The complexity of the investigation caused the trail to become colder with each passing week. The numerous tragedies of war soon distracted public and police attention from the "Tree Murder Riddle"; the woman remained unidentified, and the case was quietly forgotten about. Then, about six months later, mysterious graffiti began to appear in the area.

# Christmas 1943 / The first graffiti message appears.

The most well-known piece of graffiti appeared on the 200-year-old **Wychbury Obelisk** at Hagley Hall.

Some versions of the grafitti say: **"Who put Bella in the <u>witch</u> elm?"**

The first message – written in chalk on the side of a house in nearby Old Hill – read: "Who put Luebella down the wych elm?" This was the first time that a name had been connected to the deceased woman. Over the ensuing months, similar messages appeared, all written by the same hand. Gradually, they took on the same word form: "Who put Bella in the wych elm?" The graffiti rang with the implication that somebody knew who killed "Bella", but appeals by police to find the artist all proved unsuccessful. In the late 1940s, new messages started to appear, asking the same question. Was this a clue – or a taunt? The case became a whodunit that gripped the nation. The combination of the mysterious messages and the lack of an identity for the victim prompted some fanciful theories.

## DARK MAGIC

74-year-old Charles Walton was killed in 1945. It is the **longest unsolved murder** in Warwickshire's police records.

One notion that surfaced early on in the investigation was that "Bella" could have been the victim of a black magic ritual. According to anthropologist Professor Margaret Murray, the fact that "Bella"'s hand was severed from her arm and the bones scattered bore similarities to an occult ceremony known as the "Hand of Glory". She also concluded that the murder was somehow connected to another case potentially involving witchcraft – the murder of Charles Walton, who was stabbed and pinned to the ground with his own pitchfork in the nearby village of Lower Quinton. Developing the theory that witchcraft was involved, it was noted that the plant, belladonna– also known as deadly nightshade – and witch-hazel are both widely associated with the occult and, according to local legend, so is Hagley Woods. The fact that "Bella" was entombed inside a tree rather than being buried was also indicative of a ritualistic slaying, according to Professor Murray. The theory that "Bella" was executed for some crime against a coven quickly gathered steam and remains a favourite theory even today. Investigators working on the case, however, dismissed the theory, declaring that the bones from "Bella"'s hand had simply been scattered by animal predation.

## BELLA THE SPY?

During World War II, several German spies were captured in the UK. As a result, in 1953, the case of Bella and the wych elm attracted a new line of enquiry: war espionage. The *Wolverhampton Express and Star* received a letter from somebody who identified herself only as "Anna of Claverley". She claimed to have information on the identity of "Bella" and was interviewed by journalist Wilfred Byford-Jones. According to "Anna", "Bella" was a member of a spy ring seeking information about the location of local munitions factories that could then be targeted by the Luftwaffe.

"Anna" was later identified as Una Mossop, and she alleged that her RAF pilot husband, Jack Mossop, had witnessed "Bella"'s death. She said that Mossop told her that he had become involved in a spy ring along with a "Dutchman called Van Ralt". One evening, Van Ralt – accompanied by a woman Mossop believed to be "Bella" – had picked up Mossop in his car. Shortly after, Van Ralt strangled the woman, allegedly because of her spy associations.

Another version of this story claims that Jack Mossop and Van Ralt had been drinking with "Bella" in a local pub when she became drunk and passed out. The two men then placed the woman in the tree to teach her a lesson. When she awoke, she was unable to climb out and perished. However, this theory doesn't explain the discovery of the taffeta stuffed inside her mouth. Whichever version was reported to the newspaper has become obscured by time, but what is known is that Jack Mossop died in St. George's Hospital, Stafford, before "Bella"'s body was discovered. Allegedly, recurring nightmares of "Bella"'s skull stuffed inside the tree ultimately led to his mental breakdown. Van Ralt was never found, and investigators considered Mossop's testimony to be nothing more than hearsay from an estranged wife, told 12 years after the discovery of "Bella".

In later years, declassified MI5 files gave some weight to the spy theory. The files revealed information concerning a German spy named Josef Jakobs, who was captured after breaking his ankle while parachuting into Cambridgeshire in 1941.[1] After Jakobs' arrest, a creased photograph of the glamorous German actress and cabaret singer, Clara Bauerle, was found in his pocket. Jakobs told his interrogators that Bauerle was his lover and that the Third Reich had recruited her as a spy. According to Jakobs, Bauerle had parachuted into the West Midlands in 1941 and disappeared. Could Bauerle have been the woman Una Mossop had mentioned? Josef Jakobs was never able to shed any more light into Bauerle's fate as he was executed by firing squad in August 1941. However, it is certain that Clara Bauerle could not have been "Bella", for the simple reason that Bauerle was tall, around 1.78 metres (5 ft 10 in), whereas "Bella" was only 1.52 metres (5 ft) in height. Finally, in 2016, it was discovered that Clara Bauerle had died in a Berlin hospital in December 1942.

**Josef Jakobs** was convicted of espionage under the Treachery Act 1940. He was the last man to be executed at the Tower of London.

## LOST TO TIME

Alongside all of these imaginative theories, there was speculation that "Bella" may have been someone with a transient lifestyle—a person not easily traced in life and thus not particularly missed in death. In August 2014, BBC Radio 4 broadcast a program[2] that suggested that "Bella" was a prostitute who worked the streets around Hagley Road. According to police files, "Bella" had disappeared in 1941, which would fit the timeline of events. Locals pointed out the fact that gypsies had camped out in the vicinity of Hagley Woods during 1941. Perhaps "Bella" was one of them and had been killed by a member of her own community. Yet another suggestion was that "Bella" was a local barmaid who had been killed by an American GI.

With no concrete evidence to support them, these various theories ultimately led nowhere. One straightforward – and perhaps most probable – hypothesis is that "Bella" was a homeless woman with no loved ones to report her missing. Quite simply, she may have been a woman who just fell through the cracks.

In 2018, a team from Liverpool John Moores University used photographs of "Bella"'s skull to create a **digital impression** of how she may have looked while still alive.

As the decades passed, the mystery continued to grow. The sinister-looking tree, the severed hand and whispers of witchcraft and espionage have combined to weave this tragic tale of an anonymous woman's murder into a darkly fascinating legend.

# DEATH OF A DREAMER

**She longed to become an actress – a Hollywood star. However, a very different sort of fame lay in store for the pretty, raven-haired girl, universally remembered in the history of crime as the Black Dahlia.**

The morning of 15 January 1947, was dreary and chilly when Los Angeles housewife Betty Bersinger set off for a shoe repair shop with her 3-year-old daughter, Anne. On South Norton Avenue, they passed eerie, abandoned lots, overgrown with brush and weeds. Something white caught Betty's eye. At first she thought it was a tossed-aside mannequin, discarded perhaps because it was broken in half. Then she realised the two halves were the body of a woman. "I was terribly shocked and scared to death," Betty later told a reporter.[1] She grabbed her daughter and rushed to the first house that had a phone.

The woman that Betty and her daughter discovered would quickly become a household name as newspapers across the country detailed every twist and turn in the search for her elusive killer. Her name was Elizabeth Short, a young woman who had gone to California hoping for stardom, only to achieve it after her gruesome death. It was those two elements – the glamorous Hollywood dreams and the lurid details of Elizabeth's murder – that catapulted the case into the public's

*Opposite page, main images:* A police mugshot of Elizabeth Short, taken after her arrest for underage drinking on 23 September 1943; a glamorous publicity shot of Elizabeth.
*Opposite page, clockwise from center:* Suspect Leslie Dillon; suspect George Hodel; suspect Robert "Red" Manley taking a life detector test.

I Will

Fold-Express

Dahlia KILL

UP IN

I Get

10 Year

1 VICTIM | 11 KEY SUSPECTS

DON'T TO Find Me
TRY TO Fin

consciousness like few others before it. The young woman had been sliced carefully in half, drained of her blood and then posed in a bizarre spread-eagle display among the weeds. Rope marks scarred her ankles, wrists and throat, and police believed that she had been hung upside down by her feet and tortured for hours before her death. Her mouth had also been slashed into a grotesque, too-wide smile. As the *Los Angeles Times* reported:

"**The victim of one of the city's most brutal killings, according to veteran detectives, the attractive brunette could have died from head wounds, a deep stab wound in the abdomen, frenzied slashings in the back or from strangulation, investigators said. Jagged knife wounds also were found on the breasts and the left leg and running from the mouth across the face.**"[2]

Those who knew her could not imagine how this became the fate of the girl they affectionately called Beth or Bette. Elizabeth Short was born in Hyde Park, Massachusetts, in July 1924, to Phoebe Mae Sawyer and Cleo Short. Even as a child, she stood out with her raven hair and gray-green eyes. Her small nose was slightly upturned. The only physical flaws noted in death were a few surgical scars, chewed fingernails and bad lower teeth.

"She always wanted to be an actress," said Phoebe the week after Elizabeth's death. "She was ambitious and beautiful and full of life, but she had her moments of despondency. Sometimes she would be gay and carefree, then in the depths of despair."[3] Such swings are not unusual for some young women, but Elizabeth's early home life was troubled. Her father lost most of his life savings in the 1929 market crash and abandoned his family the following year. Phoebe was left to raise her five daughters alone. The fatherless family moved to Medford, Massachusetts, where Phoebe worked as a bookkeeper. Elizabeth struggled with asthma and recurring bronchitis, and a suggestion to move to a more hospitable climate led her to happily drop out of high school in 1943 and head to California to pursue her acting dreams. She stayed for a few months with her father in Vallejo,

Police suspected that the killer might be a **doctor** because the bisection was so precise.

Before her death, Elizabeth had been working as a **waitress**.

Elizabeth's mother told reporters that her daughter wrote to her at least **once a week**.

Cleo supposedly abandoned his **car** near a bridge, causing many to believe he had committed suicide.

Elizabeth attended the **Methodist Church** in Medford.

California, but the reunion was not happy. He claimed that she would not stay home so "I told her to go her way, I'd go mine". He never spoke to her again.[4]

By 1947, 22-year-old Elizabeth had made something of a home in San Diego. She appeared occasionally as a movie extra and auditioned for acting jobs whenever she could. She "loved to see, and be seen, in the movie colony spotlights", one friend said. Her roommates and friends told police that she had several suitors.

## MEDIA FRENZY

The media frenzy that engulfed Elizabeth's death cannot be understated. Her face was featured time and again on the front pages of newspapers across the country. "The case itself took on a life of its own," said Los Angeles Police Detective Brian Carr, who oversaw the case between 2000 and 2009.[5] Reporters soon began calling Elizabeth "The Black Dahlia", a sensational moniker bestowed in part as a nod to the then-popular movie *The Blue Dahlia*, and because of her dark hair and fondness for black clothing.

# "IT WAS FRONT-PAGE NEWS IN ALL THE LOCAL PAPERS EVERY DAY."

LOS ANGELES POLICE DETECTIVE BRIAN CARR

Every development in the case – no matter how fruitless – seemed to warrant breathless coverage. When Elizabeth's friend said she had bragged about being friends with the famous actress Ann Todd, the wire service United Press International announced that police would question the British star. Todd told police she had never met the slain starlet.

One suspect after another was arrested, each getting a guilty man's treatment for a day. 25-year-old Robert "Red" Manley, a married salesman, had been dating Elizabeth and, according to her roommates, had threatened her. He had driven her from San Diego to Los Angeles a week before her death.

---

When Elizabeth's **father** learned of her murder, he told police, "I want nothing to do with this."

Elizabeth was set to **marry** USAF Major Matthew Michael Gordon, but he died in an airplane crash in 1945.

The first reference to the **nickname** appeared two days after the discovery of the body. An article credited her boyfriends with giving her this moniker.

Elizabeth was arrested for underage drinking in Santa Barbara in September 1943. Her **fingerprints** were taken, enabling police to quickly identify her body.

Police interviewed more than **150** suspects, but none were charged.

# 9 January 1947 / Robert Manley is the last known person to see Elizabeth Short alive.

Newspapers nationwide ran a photo of Manley taking a polygraph lie-detector test. Twenty-nine-year-old Army Cpl. Joseph Dumais was also said to have been dating Elizabeth shortly before her death. Interest in him was piqued because he said that he "blacked out" after their date and had no memory of what happened to her. Both leads fell apart when each man provided alibis that checked out.

Having drawn a blank so far, police shifted focus to the women in Elizabeth's life. Could the killer have been the girlfriend or wife of one of Elizabeth's lovers? Indeed, Elizabeth's sex life was the undercurrent in many stories, with reporters and officials alike dwelling on the tawdry subject – and passing judgment. "The averages may have caught up with Beth Short. She may have picked up one man too many," was the observation of police psychiatrist Dr Paul De River. [7]

The killer then reached out to the police, sending a letter created from words and letters cut from various newspapers and magazines. The creepy correspondence read: HERE! IS DAHLIA'S BELONGINGS. Enclosed were Elizabeth's birth certificate, her address book and other personal papers. A few days later, more of her belongings – a shoe and a bag – were found in a rubbish dump. The killer sent a letter to the *Examiner* telling police where he would turn himself in. However, he never showed up. He sent another letter: "Have changed my mind. You would not give me a square deal. Dahlia killing was justified." [8] Strangely, several innocent people – both men and women – did turn themselves in. By 1996, police had fielded about 500 such confessions.

Sightings of Elizabeth in the days prior to her murder all proved false. Her **movements** between January 9 and the discovery of her body are a mystery.

A 15-year-old girl named **Lynn Martin**, who'd once roomed with Elizabeth, didn't provide much insight, but she did help sell newspapers: the caption with her photo called her "shapely" and "mature looking".

Several of those making **false** confessions were charged with obstruction of justice.

*Left:* Elizabeth Short's fingerprints from a prior arrest enabled officers to identify her body.

# I Will GiVE UP IN Dahlia KILLing if I Get 10 Years

## DON'T TRY TO Find Me

*Left:* The killer's letter to *The Examiner*, received January 23, 1947

## THE BELLHOP

In January 1949, a bellhop named Leslie Dillon contacted Dr De River, saying he wanted to discuss the murder for a book he hoped to write. De River immediately grew suspicious. Dillon had previously worked as a mortician's assistant – meaning he knew how to drain blood from a body, as had been done with Elizabeth's corpse – and "without prompting, Dillon revealed details of the crime which police have never been able to explain," said LAPD Detective Lt. Harry Hansen.[9] After questioning, Dillon implicated his friend Jeff Connors, who police interviewed but released. Investigators refocused on Dillon, and he was set to appear in late 1949 before a grand jury; however, the case was dismissed when a judge ruled that Dillon had been illegally detained.

In 2017, British author Piu Eatwell presented a theory that Dillon had orchestrated the Black Dahlia murder with his friend Connors and Mark Hansen, a local nightclub and cinema owner. Hansen was known to frequently bed chorus girls and wannabe actresses, despite being married. He was linked to Elizabeth because he had given her a place to stay in the months before her death. Eatwell suggested that Hansen had connections within the police department – connections that had enabled the trio to get away with murder.[10]

The police described **Leslie Dillon** as their "best suspect yet".

An **address book** bearing Mark Hansen's name was found among Elizabeth's possessions.

77

## SINS OF THE FATHER

More than 70 years after the crime, investigators continue to wade through countless theories. Most can be discounted, but one of the most intriguing comes from a former homicide detective who claims to have figured out the killer's identity: his own father.

Los Angeles Police Department veteran Steve Hodel began suspecting his father, a respected Los Angeles doctor, after his stepmother gave him a small photo album that belonged to the elder Hodel after his death in 1999. The book, which measured just 7.6 cm (3 in) square, contained black-and-white photographs, many of which Steve Hodel recognised. Then he came upon two images of a black-haired woman he did not know. After painstakingly comparing facial contours and counting freckles, Steve Hodel became convinced that the photos were of the notorious Black Dahlia. "I loved my father and respected him," Steve Hodel told an Associated Press reporter in 2003. "His blood flows through my body. He gave me being. But now I have come to look at my father as the true Dr Jekyll and Mr Hyde."[11] Hodel laid out his suspicions in a bestselling book, *Black Dahlia Avenger: A Genius for Murder*.[12]

According to case files released 50 years after the slaying, Dr George Hodel was indeed a suspect in Elizabeth's murder. Police electronically surveilled his home for three weeks in 1950. Soon after, the Black Dahlia case was mentioned in court when Hodel was tried for committing incest with his daughter. (He was acquitted of the charge.) Transcripts of overheard conversations included Hodel saying: "Supposin' I did kill the Black Dahlia. They couldn't prove it now. They can't talk to my secretary anymore because she's dead." At another point, Hodel also suggested he might have killed his secretary.

Why police didn't pursue Hodel is unclear. Officials have repeatedly declined to comment because the Black Dahlia investigation – while ice cold – is still technically open. "I don't have the time to either prove or disprove Hodel's investigation," said LAPD Det. Brian Carr in a 2006 episode of the television series *Cold Case Files*. "I am too busy working on active cases."

## THE LIST GROWS

Hodel was not the first to accuse his own father of being the infamous killer. In 1995, a woman named Janice Knowlton released a book called *Daddy Was the Black Dahlia Killer*. She said that her deceased father, George, not only killed Elizabeth, but that she had witnessed the murder as a 10-year-old child. She claimed she had been brought to Elizabeth's house during her father's affair with the raven-haired starlet, and that police documents indicating that they had sought a man named "George" as a suspect further implicated her father.

Another doctor was put forward as a possible suspect. Larry Harnisch, a *Los Angeles Times* copy editor, suggested that a man named Walter Bayley could have been the killer. Bayley was a surgeon who, until he left his wife some four months before the murder, had lived one block from the lot in which Elizabeth's body was dumped. Harnisch became convinced Bayley was a viable suspect after learning that one of the doctor's daughters was good friends with Elizabeth's sister, Virginia. According to Harnisch, Bayley left his wife for another woman – a fellow doctor named Alexandra von Partyka. Alexandra allegedly ended up blackmailing the doctor because she knew a secret about him – possibly that he was the Black Dahlia killer.

According to one of the countless websites dedicated to tracking the case, at least eight men are still labeled people of interest in one fashion or another. They include *Los Angeles Times* publisher Norman Chandler, who some allege had dated Elizabeth; a medical doctor named Patrick O'Reilly who allegedly met Elizabeth through nightclub owner Mark Hansen – and who was once convicted of sexual assault against his secretary; and an unidentified, dark-haired man pictured with Elizabeth in an undated photo found in the trunk of her car.

With today's advances in forensic science, it is feasible that evidence in Elizabeth's case could have been tested to get a solid new lead and find the killer once and for all. However, that is no longer possible. Over the years, physical evidence in one of the highest-profile cases in California history has gone missing. Unless it is somehow recovered, the Black Dahlia mystery is destined to endure.

---

After Knowlton died in 2004, her **stepsister** insisted that her memories were faulty and her book was "trash".[13]

Some commentators have linked the Black Dahlia case with the **Cleveland Torso Murders** of the 1930s.

A 38-year-old cowboy named **Edward Glen Thorpe** supposedly had blood in his car and had mumbled about cutting up a girl while on a bus.

Following the Black Dahlia murder, California became the first US state to create a mandatory **sex offenders registry**.

# DID SAM DO IT?

**Dr Sam Sheppard and his wife, Marilyn, seemed to have an ideal home and marriage – until a savage murder revealed the dark undercurrents in their "perfect life".**

The murder of Marilyn Sheppard and the subsequent trial of her prosperous, good-looking doctor husband has cast a long shadow. The novelist Ernest Hemingway wrote: "A trial like this, with its elements of doubt, is the greatest human story of all... This is the real thing. This trial has everything the public clamors for."

As day broke on 4 July 1954, Marilyn Sheppard was bludgeoned to death with an unknown instrument in the bedroom of the couple's idyllic home. With her husband the prime suspect, the shocking murder led to one of the longest and most controversial murder investigations and trials in American legal history.

## A PERFECT EVENING

Osteopath Dr Sam Sheppard lived in a two-storey, Dutch Colonial home in the leafy suburb of Bay Village, Ohio, overlooking Lake Erie. His wife, Marilyn, was a Sunday school teacher, and they had a young son, Samuel, nicknamed Chip. Marilyn was four months pregnant with their second child. On the evening of 3 July 1954, Sam and Marilyn were entertaining neighbours. They ate dinner together before

*Opposite page, main images:* Marilyn and Sam Sheppard on their wedding day in 1945.
*Opposite page, clockwise from top:* The crime scene; Sam Sheppard in a neck brace during his trial for murder; Susan Hayes, Sheppard's lover; witnesses Esther Houk and J. Spencer Houk, the Sheppards' Bay Village neighbours.

1 VICTIM | 2 KEY SUSPECTS | 1 WITNESS

watching the sun set over Lake Erie. At dusk, they went indoors to watch the 1945 movie *Strange Holiday.* Dr Sheppard, exhausted from a busy day at his surgical practice, later dozed off in a daybed in the living room. The neighbours left around midnight, and Marilyn went upstairs to their bedroom, leaving her husband asleep. She removed her nail polish and went to bed, leaving the bedside light on in case he woke up and came upstairs. When he was working late, Marilyn would often leave the light on for his late-night return. What happened next has shocked and baffled the world for over half a decade.

## INTRUDER TERROR

According to Sheppard, he was awoken at approximately 4:00 a.m. by Marilyn screaming his name. He added: "It wasn't actually a scream. I can't really explain it." He said that he ran upstairs to the bedroom, where he grappled with "a white form" before being struck on the back of the head and knocked out. When Sheppard regained his senses, he heard noises downstairs. He rushed to where the noise was coming from and discovered a "bushy-haired man" running away from the house. He pursued this intruder through the garden and down to the shores of the lake, where a struggle ensued. During this altercation, Sheppard was knocked unconscious once again.

When he came to, the man was gone. Sheppard ran back to the house to check on his wife and son, relieved to find that Chip was sleeping soundly and had been seemingly undisturbed through the entire ordeal. However, when Sheppard entered his and Marilyn's bedroom, he found the body of his wife sprawled on the bed, her brown hair matted in a puddle of her own blood. She had been attacked with such force and hit repeatedly – later estimated to be between 27 and 35 times – that the bones below her eye and around her mouth were detached from her face. Her nose was broken, two teeth were missing and a nail on her left hand had been torn away, presumably when she was desperately trying to defend herself against her attacker. Her pyjama top was lifted up above her breasts, and her underwear had been removed and was dangling from her right leg. The bedroom walls were spattered with blood.

Dr Sheppard had **no open wounds** when he was examined by a doctor following the murder.

Marilyn Sheppard's **front teeth** had been snapped off at the gum during the attack, indicating that she may have bitten her killer.

Police found Sam's **desk drawers** pulled open, but no items were missing. Sam's doctor's bag was also overturned, but again, nothing was missing.

## THE SHEPPARD HOME

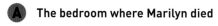

**Second floor**

**Main floor**

**A** The bedroom where Marilyn died

**B** Chip Sheppard's room

**C** The daybed where Sheppard slept

**D** Sam's study

**E** The garage

As news of the gruesome murder made headlines across the country, Leo Stawicki – a neighbour of the Sheppards – contacted police to inform them that he had spotted a strange man near the Sheppards' home in the early hours of the day that Marilyn was killed. He said he noticed the man as he was returning from a fishing trip in Sandusky at around 2:30 a.m. As his headlights illuminated the road, Leo saw him standing in the road in front of the Sheppards' house. He described the man as tall, bushy-haired, and wearing a white shirt. This description matched the one given by Sam of the man he had fought with in the bedroom and later on the shore front. Two more witnesses, Richard and Betty Knitter, would later testify that they had also seen a man with bushy hair outside the Sheppard home at around 3:00 a.m. "He had a terrified look on his face," Richard said.

Nevertheless, the police soon announced that they had essentially ruled out any theory of a "casual" intruder. Although a doctor had concluded that Dr Sheppard couldn't have inflicted the wounds he sustained on himself, investigators now suspected that he had fabricated the story of the fracas with an intruder and had killed his wife himself. The Sheppards' son had remained asleep next door during the entire attack, and it seemed that the family dog, Koko, remained silent throughout the night.

Investigators noted that **sports trophies** belonging to both Sam and Marilyn had been damaged. However, this could have been done before the day of the murder.

## TRIAL BY NEWSPAPER

To make matters worse for Sheppard, conservative Cleveland was shocked by revelations that his marriage was not as happy as it at first appeared, and that the doctor had had at least one extramarital affair – which he initially denied. Newspapers began to run headlines such as: "Why Isn't Sam Sheppard in Jail?"[1]

Two weeks after Marilyn's murder, Dr Sheppard was arrested, and the first trial began in Ohio on 18 October 1954. Newspapers and TV stations covered it extensively; the judge, Edward J. Blythin, admitted to one newspaper columnist his belief that Dr Sheppard was "guilty as hell" before any evidence was even presented. The upper-class lifestyle of the Sheppards added an element of glamour to the already sensational trial; it was to the 1950s what the O. J. Simpson trial would become to the 1990s.

The **"other woman"** in Sheppard's life was medical technician Susan Hayes. She testified that Sheppard loved Marilyn but "not as a wife" and was contemplating a divorce.

# 21 December 1954 / Dr Sheppard is convicted of murder but proclaims his innocence to the court.

During the trial, the prosecution claimed that there were no signs of forced entry to the house. A report listing a damaged door in the basement was not disclosed. Trauma expert Dr William Fallon described Sheppard's serious neck injuries as "almost impossible to self-inflict", owing to the position and severity of them. He had a fracture of the vertebrae, as well as swelling at the bottom of the skull. Despite the fact that the prosecution's case against Sheppard was entirely

A damaged **flashlight** that could have been the murder weapon was found in Lake Erie.

There was **no evidence** that Sheppard had ever physically abused his wife in the past.

circumstantial, he was convicted of second-degree murder. Some might say that he was accused of murder but convicted of adultery.

However, Sheppard's conviction was not the end of the story. Interest in the case revived in 1957 when a convict named Donald J. Welder confessed to the murder. Police dismissed his claim as fantasy; nevertheless Sheppard's legal team continued to make numerous appeals. Sheppard was finally released on bond in 1964, after serving nine years. On 6 June 1966, the Supreme Court overturned the conviction. Lambasting the "carnival atmosphere" of the original trial, the court ruled that the judge had failed to shield jurors and witnesses from the biased media circus surrounding the case.

## BACK IN COURT

A new trial was ordered, beginning on 24 October 1966. Expert Dr Paul Leland Kirk testified that Marilyn was murdered by a left-handed killer; Sheppard was right-handed. The court did not find Sheppard guilty, but neither did it declare him innocent. When Sheppard was released, the rules under which the press could report criminal trials in the US were rewritten to prevent another "trial by newspaper" ever happening again. Dr Sam Sheppard wrote a book about the case, published in 1966, titled *Endure and Conquer: My Twelve-Year Fight for Vindication*. The teaser page bore the heading: "Did Sam Do It?"[2]

# 13 April 2000/ The jury delivers its verdict in a civil suit brought by Sheppard's son, Samuel.

Sam married German divorcee Ariane Tebbenjohanns **three days** after he was released from prison. They divorced in 1969, and he married a woman named Colleen Strickland that same year.

In 2000, a civil case was filed by Sheppard's son, Samuel Reese Sheppard, in an attempt to clear his father's name. By this point, Dr Sheppard had been deceased for 30 years, but his son was determined to have him posthumously declared innocent. If the State of Ohio declared Dr Sheppard innocent, then Samuel could have sued the state for the wrongful conviction of his father. Over the 10-week trial, 76 witnesses were called and hundreds of exhibits were displayed.

## THE BUSHY-HAIRED MAN

During the 2000 trial, plaintiff attorney Terry Gilbert offered another suspect for the murder: Richard Eberling. The owner of Dick's Cleaning Services, Eberling was regularly hired by the Sheppards to wash their windows. He suffered from seizures and temper tantrums and was often caught lying and stealing. He started to lose his hair as a young adult, prompting him to wear hairpieces. In addition, Eberling had been convicted in 1989 of killing Ethel Mae Durkin – an elderly widow – as part of a fraudulent scheme to collect on her will.

Eberling was first connected to the murder of Marilyn Sheppard in 1959, when he was arrested for a string of robberies on Cleveland's west side. Many of the houses that he targeted belonged to his window cleaning clients, and tens of thousands of dollars' worth of items were stolen. One piece of particular interest to police was a diamond ring, which Eberling kept apart from the other items he accumulated. This ring once belonged to Marilyn Sheppard. Eberling claimed that he had stolen it from Dr Sheppard's brother's home, where he found a box marked "Property of Marilyn Sheppard".

Eberling went on to tell police that just days before Marilyn's murder, he had cut his finger while changing storm windows and that he had dripped blood throughout the Sheppards' home. Was he anticipating the need for an alibi? In February 1997, DNA in the blood found on the stairs, as well as semen found on Marilyn, was consistent with Eberling's DNA. This DNA type was shared by approximately 5 percent of the population. Bay Village police had wanted to pursue him as a suspect at the time, but Cuyahoga County Prosecutor John T. Corrigan and Coroner Samuel R. Gerber considered the case closed.

Adding more weight to the evidence against Eberling, Robert Lee Parks – a convicted robber who was incarcerated with Eberling – told police that Eberling had confessed that he killed Marilyn and that everything Dr Sheppard had said about the "bushy-haired intruder" was true. Eberling allegedly told Parks that he had gone to the Sheppards' home to rob it and to rape Marilyn, thinking that Dr Sheppard was working late. He also admitted that he was wearing a

Eberling had had a **difficult upbringing**, having been in and out of five foster homes by the age of 7.

There was speculation that Eberling was involved in his **foster father's death** in 1946, when he was just 16 years old.

Eberling said that he had lunch with Marilyn Sheppard in her home **two days** before her murder. He called her a "lovely, lovely lady".[3]

Blood was found on a closet door in Marilyn's bedroom. During the civil trial, a **DNA expert** said he was 90 percent sure one spatter belonged to Richard Eberling, but this evidence was not admissible.

Blood from a **third person** was found on the pants Dr. Sheppard was wearing at the time of the murder. It has never been identified.

bushy-haired wig and makeup. Eberling apparently killed Marilyn when she bit him and screamed for help while he raped her. Even though no blood in the house matched the DNA profile of Dr Sheppard and instead matched Eberling – who was also found in possession of Marilyn's ring – the jury sided with county prosecutors and declared that they could not find Dr Sheppard posthumously innocent of his wife's murder.

## FURTHER SUSPICIONS

While Dr Sheppard and Richard Eberling remain the two main suspects, former FBI agent Bernard Conners, in his book *Tailspin: The Strange Case of Major Call*, contends that Air Force Maj. James Arlon Call killed Marilyn during a cross-country crime spree, which ended in a deadly shoot-out with police in Lake Placid, New York. Conners points to a bite wound on Call's hand, which he believes was inflicted by Marilyn during their struggle. Conners also believes that the murder weapon was a crowbar found in Call's possession.

F. Lee Bailey, the lawyer who won Dr Sheppard's second acquittal, presented Spencer and Esther Houk, neighbours of the Sheppards, as suspects. The motivation, he claimed, was that Esther caught her husband and Marilyn having an affair and killed Marilyn in a fit of rage. Bailey's theory was presented to a grand jury but they decided against indicting the Houks, who had been dead for years.

Esther Houk and J. Spencer Houk were **first on the scene** when Marilyn was killed.

The murder of Marilyn Sheppard gave rise to many books, inspired a hit 1960s TV series and a 1993 movie (both called *The Fugitive*), and led to a precedent-setting Supreme Court decision on the effects of pretrial publicity, ensuring the case a prominent place in popular culture and legal history. The "trial of the century" never proved who killed Marilyn Sheppard, leaving the case still unsolved. Following Sheppard's release, many still considered him guilty. He lived under a cloud of suspicion and was barred from the medical profession. He fell into a haze of alcohol and drugs, and died in 1970 at the age of just 46. The cause of death was liver failure. His son, however, said the true cause was "a broken heart and a spirit that found no solace".

After failing to reenter the medical profession, Sheppard became a **professional wrestler** under the name of "Killer" Sam Sheppard.

# THE LAST BIKE RIDE

**A tragic series of events followed by a biased police investigation resulted in a 14-year-old boy becoming the youngest-ever inmate on Canada's Death Row.**

The murder of Lynne Harper and subsequent arrest of a 14-year-old boy contains many of the hallmarks of a wrongful conviction. The investigation focused on Steven Truscott as the main suspect; evidence was corrupted to look incriminating, and at a time when people had uncritical attitudes towards the justice system, he was convicted of her murder with almost no questions asked. Since then, however, some highly questionable police work has come to light and the science that found the teenager guilty has been thoroughly discredited. But if Steven Truscott was wrongly accused over half a century ago, then who really killed Lynne Harper?

## SUMMER BIKE RIDE

It was the summer of 1959, and Steven Truscott's father was stationed at Clinton Air Force Base in Clinton, Ontario. The teenager attended the Air Vice Marshal Hugh Campbell School located on the north side of the base. It was here that he met 12-year-old Lynne Harper, the daughter of an officer at the Clinton base. On 9 June 1959, Lynne had dinner with her family before going outside at around 6:15 p.m. It was

*Opposite page, main images:* Lynne Harper; the crime scene in Lawson's Bush.
*Opposite page, top to bottom:* Provincial Police Commissioner Harold Graham, who arrested Steven Truscott in 1959; Steven Truscott leaving the Supreme Court after cross-examination in 1966; 14-year-old Steven Truscott after his arrest.

1 VICTIM | 1 BIKE RIDE | 6 KEY SUSPECTS

a pleasant summer evening and the sun had not yet set. According to Steven, he started chatting with Lynne outside their school at around 7:00 p.m. He said that she asked if he could give her a ride on his bicycle to Highway 8, where she planned to hitchhike to a quaint white house just north of the highway. The owner of the house kept ponies and Lynne loved ponies. Steven agreed, Lynne perched herself on the handlebars of his bicycle and off they went. Several witnesses would later state that they spotted the pair cycling on a country road running alongside the Bayfield River, a popular spot for swimming and fishing, which was on the way to Highway 8.

What happened next is the crux of the case. Steven asserts that he dropped Lynne off on Highway 8 and as he glanced back while cycling towards Bayfield Bridge, he saw her climb into a "late model Chevrolet" with yellow plates. The car then drove east. Others have argued that, instead, Steven took Lynne into nearby woodland known as Lawson's Bush, where he raped and strangled her.

## DISCOVERING THE BODY

When Lynne didn't return home that night, her worried father called police to report her missing. A search party was swiftly assembled, and an extensive search for the young girl ensued. Two days later, a search party member from the Clinton base made a terrible discovery in Lawson's Bush. Partially hidden among the foliage was the semi-naked, lifeless body of Lynne Harper. She had been raped and subsequently strangled to death with her own white, sleeveless blouse, which was still around her pale neck. Her face and chest were dotted with maggots, and larvae had gathered near the buttocks. These gruesome details, ignored at the time, would one day be used as crucial evidence.

The autopsy was conducted in a cramped and poorly lit room at a Clinton funeral home. The regional pathologist, Dr John Penistan, issued three versions of the autopsy report, all of which had a different time of death. He finally concluded that Lynne had died on 9 June between 7:15 p.m. and 7:45 p.m. The first two autopsy reports declared

The Ontario Provincial Police led a team of **250** military, police, and civilian searchers.

that she had died after 8:00 p.m., but by the time the third autopsy report was issued, police had announced that Steven Truscott was the main suspect in the slaying. In order for him to become so, the timeline of events had to be tweaked to put the time of Lynne Harper's murder *before* 8:00 p.m. This was because Steven had been seen riding his bicycle near the schoolyard at approximately 8:00 p.m. and was home shortly after that time to look after his siblings.

## STEVEN'S MOVEMENTS

**A** Steven and Lynne meet at school at about 7 p.m.

**B** Location of witnesses who see Steven and Lynne cycle across bridge

**C** Location that Steven claims Lynne got into Chevrolet

**D** Steven arrives home just after 8 p.m.

**E** Lynne's body found on 11 June

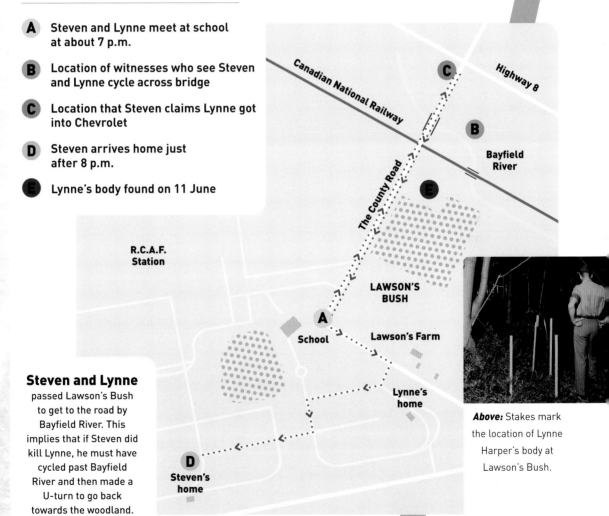

**Steven and Lynne**
passed Lawson's Bush to get to the road by Bayfield River. This implies that if Steven did kill Lynne, he must have cycled past Bayfield River and then made a U-turn to go back towards the woodland.

**Above:** Stakes mark the location of Lynne Harper's body at Lawson's Bush.

# 12 June 1959 / Steven Truscott is arrested for the murder of Lynne Harper.

## TEENAGER ON TRIAL

Steven Truscott was arrested and put on trial for the murder of his schoolfriend, strongly protesting his innocence the entire time. The time of Lynne Harper's death and Steven's whereabouts remained two key issues at his trial. Ultimately, the courtroom testimony of Dr Penistan was comparable to a noose tightening around Steven's neck. The doctor claimed that the murder had occurred between 7:00 p.m. and 7:45 p.m., when Lynne Harper had been in the company of Steven. He based this assertion on the fact that he had found a full meal in Lynne Harper's stomach, the stomach normally takes two hours to empty, and her last meal had been at 5.45 p.m. Subsequent medical research, however, has shown that the stomach may take up to six hours to empty.

Despite a total lack of physical evidence against him, Steven Truscott was found guilty and sentenced to hang. His death sentence was commuted to life in prison in 1960, the same year that his first appeal was denied. In 1966, the Supreme Court of Canada upheld his conviction; three years later, Steven was released on parole. Following his release, he went on to marry and have three children while living under an assumed name. He kept a low profile until 2000 when his case was featured on the CBC TV investigative documentary *The Fifth Estate*, which portrayed the trial as a miscarriage of justice. In 2001, the Association in Defence of the Wrongfully Convicted successfully filed an appeal to have the case reopened.

## A QUESTION OF TIMING

In 2006, five judges of the Ontario Court of Appeal began a landmark review of the case and Steven Truscott stood trial once again in a bid to clear his name. Much of the proceedings focused on evidence that was unavailable to his lawyers at his original trial.

One of the defense witnesses, 12-year-old Gordon Logan, testified that he had seen Steven and Lynne cross **Bayfield Bridge,** and Steven return alone about five minutes later.

Most of the witnesses who claimed to have seen Lynne and Steven cross the bridge were **children**. The Crown dismissed some as liars.

Dr Michael Pollanen, Ontario's chief pathologist, took the stand to announce that in his opinion, the original pathologist did not have enough evidence to support his finding that Lynne Harper had died within a 45-minute window on the night of 9 June 1959. Dr Pollanen said that "the time of death window must be broadened to include June 9 and June 10".[1] Blowflies, maggots, and insect activity on the body raised reasonable doubts that she died as early as the original pathologist had determined. During the 1950s, forensic entomology – the study of insects and decomposition – was practically nonexistent. Despite this, the insects were thankfully still collected at the time. Knowing when insects deposit their eggs or larvae on a corpse gives a clearer estimation of the time of death; the maggots and larvae found on Lynne's body were in the first stage of development. Forensic entomologist Gail Anderson concluded that the insects began to colonise on Lynne's body on 10 June, indicating that she had been killed much later than previously claimed.

Truscott's story about his last moments with Lynne Harper were also readressed in the Ontario Court of Appeal. During the 1959 trial, Lynne's parents had insisted that their daughter would never hitchhike, refuting his account. However, Catherine Beamer – who had been a close friend of both Lynne and Steven – stated that hitchhiking was common, and that she and Lynne had done it "at least 15 to 20 times".

New testimony that harmed the defence came from one of the original witnesses, Karen Daum. In 1959, Daum (who was 9 years old at the time) told police that she had seen Steven and Lynne near the railway tracks – north of Lawson's Bush – at about 7:15 p.m. However, in 2006, she testified that she had actually seen the pair further south. She recalled that Truscott had veered towards her, causing her to fall off her bike into a ditch south of the trail leading to Lawson's Bush.

**Daum** had given a written statement to the police, but was never called to testify at the 1959 trial.

## SUSPECTS REVEALED

At the Ontario Court of Appeal, the defence argued that once the local police officers made Steven Truscott their prime suspect, the murder investigation ground to a halt, and other leads and tips were ignored.

Several alternative suspects in the case were acknowledged in the court documents but never publicly identified by name. They included a convicted pedophile who was stationed at the Clinton base at the time of the murder. This unidentified man came to the attention of the police in 1997 after a retired officer informed them that he believed the man was capable of murdering a child.

Another suspect was a former salesman who drove a 1957 Chevy and often visited the Clinton base. He first came to police attention when he broke into the home of retired detective Barry Ruhl and assaulted his wife before Ruhl overpowered and arrested him. Ruhl investigated this anonymous man and came to the conclusion that he was a suspect in several murders – including that of Lynne Harper.

Court documents also referred to a convicted rapist who lived in the nearby town of Seaforth and worked as an electrician on the Clinton base. He had visited the Harpers' home before the murder to repair a clothes dryer. Shortly after Lynne's murder, he moved to the US, where he was charged with sexual offences, for which he was acquitted.

## THE SUSPECT MINISTER

The fourth suspect mentioned in the documents was a minister who was later accused of sexual assault by his own adult daughters. One of them informed police that when she was 6 years old, she hid in her father's car when he took it out for a drive. She claimed that he stopped on a gravel road and opened the trunk. She peeked out of the window and allegedly saw him carrying the body of a girl towards some trees. About half an hour later, he returned to the car alone.

**The minister**
lived in the township of Dungannon, just 30.6 km (19 miles) north of the Clinton base.

The final suspect – and the only other one to ever be publicly identified – was an airman who had once been stationed at Clinton base. At the time of the crime, he was stationed at Aylmer and had a home in Seaford. He was an alcoholic with psychiatric problems and a sexual interest in children. Twelve days before Lynne Harper was murdered, he was released after being arrested for attempting to lure little girls to his car in nearby St. Thomas. This suspect would later be identified as Sgt. Alexander Kalichuk, who had passed away in 1975.[2] Many Clinton

**The airman**
was said to visit Clinton quite frequently.

residents believe that the military deflected blame for Lynne Harper's murder to protect its reputation and, as evidence, point to the disappearance of military records from 1959.

## THE LONG ROAD TO JUSTICE

The **Harper family** maintained the belief that Steven Truscott was guilty. When he was acquitted in 2006, Lynne's father was taken to the hospital with breathing problems.

In 2008, Truscott was awarded **$6.5 million** in compensation for his time spent behind bars.

In August 2007, Steven Truscott was acquitted of all charges. His defence team wanted him to declared "factually innocent", but the court ruled that was impossible because "in a case of circumstantial evidence like this, there is certainly nothing on this record that would lead you to the conclusion that he's factually innocent".[3] It is rare for a defendant to be declared innocent after being found guilty unless there is DNA evidence to prove beyond a reasonable doubt that another person perpetrated the crime. It was a long-awaited ending and most observers were satisfied with the outcome, altough, as Steven pointed out: "The Crown had most of this information 48 years, two months, and 19 days ago."[4] Steven remained highly critical of the legal system that had put him through so much.

# "THE CROWN CHOOSES TO NOT THINK ABOUT JUSTICE. IT WOULD ALMOST APPEAR THEY'RE MORE INTERESTED IN CONVICTIONS."

STEVEN TRUSCOTT

In 2006, Lynne's body was exhumed for further testing, in hopes that it could lead to the killer and prove Steven innocent. **No viable DNA** was retrieved.

On that hot summer's evening in 1959, Steven Truscott and Lynne Harper – perched precariously on his handlebars – cycled away from their school, onto the highway and into Canadian legal history. Any retrial is now unlikely, owing to the amount of time that has passed. Most of those involved in the case are long since dead and evidence has been lost or destroyed. The murderer that robbed Lynne Harper of her life also robbed Steven Truscott of his childhood and left him living under a cloud of suspicion for nearly half a century.

# CAMPSITE OF HORRORS

**This seemingly motiveless attack on four sleeping teenagers in a famous Finnish beauty spot has passed into the darkest annals of unexplained crime.**

Finland's beautiful Lake Bodom is situated near the southern city of Espoo. Between June and August the sun does not set, temperatures soar and Finns of all ages flock to the lake to celebrate the arrival of summer and the passing of the long, freezing winter. It was in this carefree spirit that, on 4 June 1960, four teenagers pitched their tent on the lake's tranquil shore.

Maila Irmeli Björklund and Anja Tuulikki Mäki, both 15, and their boyfriends, Seppo Antero Boisman and Nils Wilhelm Gustafsson, both 18, had planned an evening of fishing and camping. After riding their motorcycles to Lake Bodom from their hometown of Vantaa, the teenagers chose a spot shaded by birch trees along the idyllic Finnish bay. They spent the evening chatting, swimming and fishing, completely oblivious to the horrors that would soon unfold at their campsite. Between 4:00 a.m. and 6:00 a.m., the sleeping teenagers were brutally attacked. They were bludgeoned with a heavy object, possibly a large rock, and slashed and stabbed with a knife. The murder weapons would never be found.

*Opposite page, main image:* The funeral of the three Lake Bodom murder victims.
*Opposite page, clockwise from top:* One of the boys who might have seen the killer; the ripped and stained tent, one of the main exhibits at Nils Gustafsson's 2005 trial; Gustafsson, who was acquitted of all charges; suspect Hans Assmann; young Nils, sole survivor, in 1960.

**3 VICTIMS | 3 KEY SUSPECTS**

0 MURDER WEAPONS | 2 WITNESSES

The following morning, a local carpenter named Risto Sirén stumbled across the grim scene while out for a swim with his son. Miraculously, Nils was unconscious but still clinging to life. He was the sole survivor of the brutal attack, but was not without injuries. He suffered from concussion, fractures to the jaw, bruises on his face and stab wounds. When he came to, he stated that he had no recollection of the attack, owing to shock. "My last memory is of when we went to bed and wished each other good night. After that, I don't remember if it was Wednesday or Thursday when I woke up," he stated.[1] Of all of the victims, Nils' girlfriend, Maila, sustained the most vicious injuries. She was discovered lying on top of the tent with her underwear removed, and she had suffered significantly more stab wounds than the others. A cluster of wounds had been inflicted postmortem, the majority on her neck.

## MYSTERY ATTACKER

An investigation of the crime scene revealed that the killer had not entered the tent but had attacked the teenagers from outside of it as they slept. The tent had at least 25 slashes. Several items belonging to the teenagers appeared to have been stolen, including a wallet and items of clothing, including Nils' shoes. Strangely, the keys to the victims' motorcycles had been taken, but not the bikes themselves. Approximately ½ mile (800 metres) from the crime scene, several of these items were found, including Nils' shoes, which were partially hidden. In front of the mangled tent was a set of bloody footprints that matched Nils' discarded shoes, implying that the killer had fled the scene while wearing them.

Two boys who had been birdwatching near the crime scene came forward to tell police that they had seen a blond-haired man walking away from the collapsed tent at approximately 6:00 a.m. These young eyewitnesses would later undergo hypnosis in the hope that they could provide more information. While they couldn't give further details, their story remained the same, and a composite sketch of this unidentified man was drawn by a police sketch artist. After making a

# 11 a.m., 5 June 1960 / The bodies are discovered.

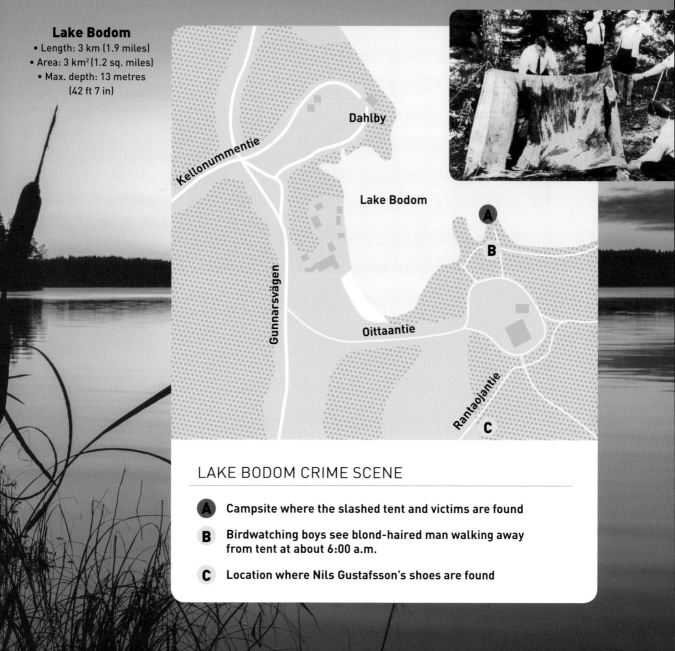

**Lake Bodom**
- Length: 3 km (1.9 miles)
- Area: 3 km² (1.2 sq. miles)
- Max. depth: 13 metres (42 ft 7 in)

Dahlby

Kellonummentie

Lake Bodom

**A**

**B**

Gunnarsvägen

Oittaantie

Rantaojantie

**C**

## LAKE BODOM CRIME SCENE

**A** Campsite where the slashed tent and victims are found

**B** Birdwatching boys see blond-haired man walking away from tent at about 6:00 a.m.

**C** Location where Nils Gustafsson's shoes are found

full recovery from his injuries, Nils would also undergo hypnosis. During his session, he recollected a vision of a figure coming towards him, clad in black and with glaring red eyes.

## THE KIOSK VENDOR

Over time, several individuals became suspects in the gruesome triple murder. One of the most plausible among the locals was Karl Valdemar Gyllström, a kiosk vendor at Lake Bodom. Karl was known for his particularly aggressive behaviour towards campers. On occasion, he would slash the ropes of tents so that they would collapse on the sleeping occupant. Ulf Johansson, the author of *Legend of Bodom*, recalled how he was once the victim of Karl's anger; when he was a teenager, Karl had thrown rocks at him as he cycled past.

# "ME AND ALL THE OTHER NORTHERNERS, WE ALWAYS KNEW WHO THE MURDERER WAS."

ULF JOHANSSON, AUTHOR OF *LEGEND OF BODOM*[2]

Many locals had found it extremely suspicious that, following the murders, Karl filled in a well on his property. Because the murder weapons had never been discovered, there were those who suspected that they had been interred in the well. In 1969, Karl drowned in Lake Bodom. He had never been fully investigated as a suspect in the murders; his wife had provided a seemingly iron-clad alibi for him, claiming that he was in bed asleep. However, shortly before his wife passed away, she confessed that this alibi was false and claimed that he had threated to kill her and their children if she refused to provide a cover story for him.

## THE MAN WITH BLOND HAIR

Another prime suspect throughout the investigation was an alleged KGB spy named Hans Assmann, who once claimed he had served as a

**Soldiers** were brought in to search the area, but in doing so, they disturbed the crime scene.

Shortly before his death, Karl allegedly **confessed** to a neighbour that he had killed the campers.

guard at Auschwitz. The day after the murders, Hans checked himself into the Helsinki Surgical Hospital, where his appearance was said to be extremely dishevelled. Nurses recollected that he had black fingernails and his clothing was stained with a red substance. The doctors who saw him that afternoon were adamant that the red stains on his clothes were blood. Moreover, Hans was said to have acted in a very suspicious manner at the hospital, giving a false name, telling contradicting stories about how he had injured himself and feigning unconsciousness.

Despite the doctors' and nurses' reports, Hans' **bloodstained clothing** was never examined by police.

After the description of the blond-haired suspect spotted by the young birdwatchers was released to the media, Hans chopped off his own blond locks. In addition, his clothing was said to match that worn by the elusive blond-haired man. Perhaps most chillingly, a man who looked strikingly similar to Hans was photographed at the funeral of the victims. It isn't unheard of for killers to make an appearance at their victims' funerals, perhaps out of morbid curiosity or with the intention of taunting investigators. Some murderers derive sadistic pleasure from knowing something that nobody else does. Despite all this powerful, admittedly circumstantial, evidence, Hans was never brought in for questioning.

Several books have been written about Hans Assman and he has been linked to several other unsolved murders, including that of 17-year-old Auli Kyllikki Saari. In 2003, Dr Jorma Palo, who had been training at the Helsinki Surgical Hospital when Hans came in for treatment, published a book in which he named Hans as the killer.[3] Allegedly while on his deathbed, Hans confessed to the murders; however, this claim cannot be verified.

## LOOK AT THE DNA

The case eventually went cold, but because Finland has no statute of limitations for murder, it was reopened in 2004. Sole-survivor Nils Gustafsson, now married with two grown-up children, was arrested on suspicion of having committed the murders. Investigators claimed that the broken jaw he had sustained during the attack was the result of a fight with Seppo, his best friend. They now believed that Nils had killed the trio and arranged the crime scene, inflicting the knife wounds and blunt force trauma on himself to give the impression of a frenzied attack by an unknown killer.

# 4 August 2005 / 45 years after the murders were committed, the trial of Nils Gustafsson begins.

Investigators announced that they had discovered a key piece of evidence that allegedly tied Nils to the murders: DNA testing had been carried out on Nils' discarded shoes that revealed traces of the victims' blood. During Nils' trial, his defence argued that the new DNA evidence didn't prove that Nils was guilty of the murders. They contended that the killer could have easily stolen and worn Nils' shoes, along with several other items of clothing that were taken. The prosecution refuted these arguments, stating that Nils had committed the murders and then discarded his shoes in an attempt to conceal his guilt.

The defence used DNA evidence of their own to strengthen their case by presenting a pillowcase that had been found inside the teenagers' tent. On it, they found sperm that didn't match either Nils or Seppo. They argued that this was evidence that somebody else had carried out the attack on the victims in a sexual frenzy. The fact that Nils' own blood was found on the inside of the tent, indicating that he, too, had been inside the tent during the frenzied attack, further strengthened their case.

## VICTIM OR KILLER?

Both the defence and the prosecution produced experts who gave conflicting statements with regard to the injuries that Nils had suffered on that fateful night. Neurology specialist Olli Tenovuo claimed it was very plausible that Nils had suffered memory loss following the attack. The prosecution called in the respected physician Eero Hirvensalo, who told the court that he believed Nils' injuries were consistent with being punched with a fist, as opposed to being bludgeoned with a heavy object. "These jaw fractures are low-energy injuries that did not require great violence," he claimed.[4] The prosecution argued that such injuries were not serious enough to cause memory loss.

Ultimately, the court agreed with the defence, accepting that the boys' eyewitness testimony of a blond-haired man departing the scene was credible. It ruled that an unknown assailant had probably attacked the four teenagers as they slept in their tent, and rejected the prosecution's scenario that a fight between Nils and Seppo had triggered the murders. The court deduced that it was very unlikely that Nils could have inflicted his wounds on himself.

# "HE WAS VERY BADLY INJURED AND COULD NOT HAVE DONE WHAT HE IS BEING CHARGED WITH."

RIITTA LEPPINIEMI, NILS' ATTORNEY

**Nils Gustafsson spent more than 500 days in custody.**

Furthermore, the court questioned how Nils could have disposed of the murder weapons in such a short time frame. Nils was duly acquitted of all charges, and was awarded €44,900 (£40, 829) compensation for the suffering his arrest and trial had caused him.

## DEEP WATERS

The Lake Bodom Murders have haunted Finland for decades, inspiring books, conspiracy theories, movies, even a death metal band named Children of Bodom. The mystery surrounding the identity of the killer or killers, as well as the killer's motive, has elevated the case to quasi-mythical status. Three generations of children have grown up being told not to stay out late for fear of the Bodom murderer. As long as the killer is unidentified, that fear shall remain.

# KILLING FOR FUN

**A callous killer, seemingly acting at random, was roaming northern California. He was also taunting the police by mailing clues to the press in a weird code of his own devising...**

In Benicia, California, a teenage couple sharing their first date parked on Lake Herman Road, a secluded lovers' lane, were startled by a beam of light. They squinted and saw a man with a flashlight, perhaps a police officer? The pair were nervous – who wouldn't be? But their fears were innocently rooted in their parents finding out they'd been caught in such an intimate setting. Then the stranger pulled out a gun. Within seconds, 17-year-old David Faraday was fatally shot in the head. 16-year-old Betty Lou Jensen desperately tried to flee and staggered only a little way away before collapsing to the ground, killed by five bullets to her back.

## THIS IS THE ZODIAC SPEAKING...

As horrific as the scene was to the sheriff's deputies who began investigating it on 20 December 1968, they were ignorant of its significance, assuming the killer must have been a jealous suitor of Betty Lou's. It would be seven months before they would learn that this double shooting marked the first murders that would be claimed by an elusive criminal known as the Zodiac Killer.

*Opposite page, main image:* Police sketches of suspects; an extract of the Zodiac Killer's code.
*Opposite page, clockwise from top:* Victims Betty Lou Jensen, David Faraday, Darlene Ferrin, Cecilia Shepard, Bryan Hartnell and Paul Stine; law enforcement officers compare notes on the case.

7 VICTIMS | 18 LETTERS | 5 KEY SUSPECTS

Most killers avoid direct contact with the police, but the Zodiac Killer was very different – he chose to deliberately taunt them. He started by sending three letters to California newspapers: the *San Francisco Chronicle*, *San Francisco Examiner* and *Vallejo Times-Herald*. The writer of these letters claimed responsibility not just for the Benicia shooting, but also another...

## THE SECOND ATTACK

Darlene Ferrin was a 22-year-old wife and mother who worked as a waitress in Vallejo, California. On 5 July 1969, she had picked up her friend, 19-year-old Michael Mageau, and parked in a secluded spot at Blue Rock Springs Park. A stranger approached with a flashlight, stuck a semiautomatic pistol through the open driver's-side window of the car and opened fire. Ferrin was killed, but despite being shot in the jaw, hip, leg and shoulder, Mageau survived – though his physical recovery would take months.

**Mageau** told police that when he cried out in pain, the assailant returned to fire two more shots at each victim before leaving them for dead.

# 31 July 1969 / The first letters from the Zodiac Killer are published in the California press.

In his letters, the Zodiac Killer not only claimed credit for the murders, he also revealed specific details that only the shooter and the investigating officers could possibly know, such as Super X being the brand of ammunition used in the Benicia killing, and Western the ammunition in the Vallejo murder. Split among the three letters was a cipher that the writer claimed would identify him. He demanded that the newspapers run the cipher in full; if they did not, he promised to go on a killing spree. Within days, the newspapers had complied. The code was a mishmash of English and Greek letters, as well as symbols from astrology, the Egyptian *Book of the Dead*, Asian mythology and from Native American rock carvings. Making it even harder to decipher were myriad misspellings and grammatical errors. Nevertheless, within a week, a high school teacher named Donald Harden had cracked the code with his wife. It read:

**The letters** included details such as David lying on his back with his feet towards the car, Betty Lou lying on her right side and Darlene wearing patterned trousers.

"I like killing people because it in [sic] more fun than killing wild game in the forrest [sic] because man is the moat dangerue anamal [sic] of all to kill something gives me the most thrilling expeerence [sic]  The best part ia thae [sic] when I die I will be reborn in paradice [sic] and all the [sic] I have killed will become my slaves [sic] I will not give you my name because you will trs [sic] to sloi [sic] down or stop my collecting of slaves for my afterlife"

The last line is still a mystery: EBEO RIET EMETH HPITI. If the killer wanted infamy, his cipher delivered in full. Psychiatrists took to TV and newspapers to offer their analyses, which included terms and phrases like "omnipotence" and "delusions of grandeur". One told the *Los Angeles Times* that the killer was most likely an isolated individual.

# "HE PROBABLY FEELS HIS FELLOW MAN LOOKS DOWN ON HIM FOR SOME REASON."
A PSYCHIATRIST IN THE *LOS ANGELES TIMES*

The same unnamed psychiatrist said if the letters and cipher had been faked, it was done by a "very, very disturbed person". If the writings were real, "the man probably will kill again". And he did.

### THE MAN IN THE MASK

Saturday, 27 September was warm and sunny – the perfect day for Cecilia Ann Shepard, 22, and Bryan Hartnell, 20, to have a picnic. Lake Berryessa Park, about 20 miles north of Napa, California, offered a picturesque scene for their evening outing as they spread out their blanket and food at a spot near the water.

At about 6:30 p.m., an ominous figure approached. The man was at least 6 feet tall, wore dark gloves and, over his head, a dark blue hood with large slits for his eyes and mouth. A peculiar image was painted on the hood: a crossed circle hand-painted in white. The man waved a pistol at them and announced that he'd escaped from a prison in

Cecilia and Bryan had **dated** during college but moved on to become friends.

**The masked man** parked his car behind Bryan Hartnell's white VW.

Montana after killing a guard. He only wanted their money and car keys so he could flee to Mexico. The couple agreed, but the man insisted on tying them up to prevent them from alerting others after he had left. He used a plastic clothesline to bind their hands behind their backs, and then between their legs. Then he calmly said he had to stab them.

"Please stab me first. I'm chicken. I couldn't stand to see her stabbed," Bryan pleaded. The masked man replied, "I'll do just that." Once Bryan passed out from a dozen knife wounds to his back, the attacker sliced Cecilia Ann as though he were frenzied – first in the back, and then flipping her over to stab her in her breasts, stomach and groin. The wounds to her front created an outline like the one painted onto his hood: the crosshairs of a gun sight. He then left a message. Scrawled onto the door of Bryan's car were words, dates and a time, each related to his attacks on David Faraday and Betty Lou Jensen, and Darlene Ferrin and Michael Mageau:

**Vallejo**

**12-20-68**

**7-4-69**

**Sept 27-69–6:30**

**by knife**

The killer wanted credit. An hour after the attack, he used a payphone outside of a car wash in Napa to call the police and report his own crime: "I want to report a murder – no, a double murder. They are 2 miles (3.2 km) north of park headquarters. They were in a white Volkswagen Karmann-Ghia. And I'm the one that did it."

## CLUES FROM THE KILLER

Two weeks later, the same man killed a cab driver named Paul Stine in San Francisco. Police likely wouldn't have suspected that the serial killer slaughtering young couples was also behind the slaying of the lone 29-year-old man, but the Zodiac Killer himself ensured that they knew exactly who the culprit was. He had torn a piece of bloodied shirt from Stine's lifeless body and, two days after the slaying, mailed it to the *San Francisco Chronicle*.

After the attack, Bryan and Cecilia managed to **untie** each other. Bryan attempted to find help, but had lost too much blood to get far.

A fisherman heard Cecilia and Bryan's **screams** and alerted park rangers.

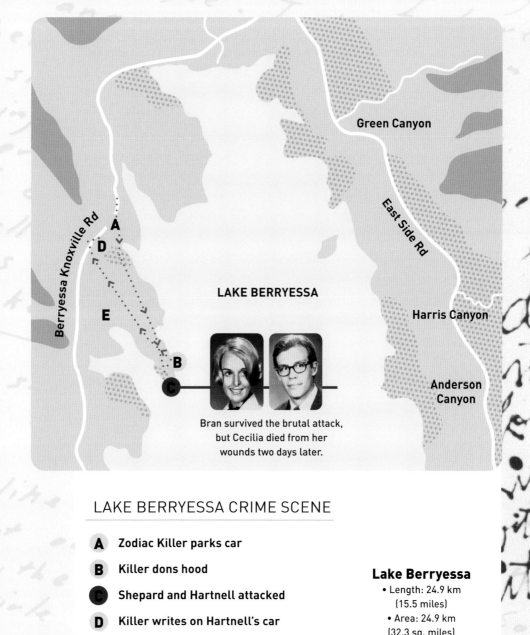

Green Canyon

East Side Rd

Berryessa Knoxville Rd

**A**

**D**

**E**

**B**

**C**

**LAKE BERRYESSA**

Harris Canyon

Anderson Canyon

Bran survived the brutal attack, but Cecilia died from her wounds two days later.

## LAKE BERRYESSA CRIME SCENE

**A** Zodiac Killer parks car

**B** Killer dons hood

**C** Shepard and Hartnell attacked

**D** Killer writes on Hartnell's car

**E** Hartnell collapses after trying to crawl for help

**Lake Berryessa**
• Length: 24.9 km
  (15.5 miles)
• Area: 24.9 km
  (32.3 sq. miles)
• Max. depth: 84 metres
  (275 ft)

By now, the killer had left behind a scattering of clues. At Lake Berryessa, police found a size-11 footprint with an unusual sole pattern. They identified the brand as having been sold at Sears. The investigators pulled fingerprints from the payphone in Napa and Stine's taxi cab. Unfortunately, their biggest break was also their biggest blunder. Three people witnessed Stine's murder and called police, providing a description of the killer: white male, 25 to 30 years old, about 1.75 metres tall (5 ft 9 in), with a stocky build. His hair was styled in a crew cut, and he wore heavy-rimmed glasses. Somehow, this information was miscommunicated and officers were told to be on the lookout for a black man. So when two cops spotted a white man matching this description walking away from the scene, they didn't bother to stop him.

The two officers later worked with a sketch artist to create a **drawing** of the man they saw. This prompted tips to pour in—but none led to an arrest.

The Zodiac Killer kept taunting in his letters, boasting that the police would never catch him because he was too smart for them. He also threatened schoolchildren, promising to shoot out the tyre of a school bus and "pick off the kiddies as they come bouncing out".[2] This terrifying threat prompted officers throughout the area to guard school buses, while volunteer teachers and parents rode inside the vehicles.

At the height of the Zodiac panic, a man identifying himself as the killer called into a television show hosted by Jim Dunbar of KGO-TV in the San Francisco Bay area. The caller insisted that he speak on air with famed attorney Melvin Belli. Over the course of two hours and more than a dozen phone calls, the caller said he was sick and suffered from headaches – and that killing alleviated the pain. Belli tried to coax him into surrendering to police. The caller at times seemed receptive, but then blurted, "I don't want to give myself up. I want to kill those kids." The entire exchange was televised.

Belli was best known for representing **Jack Ruby**, the man who shot and killed Lee Harvey Oswald, President John F. Kennedy's assassin.

Police were never able to say whether the calls were legitimate or a **hoax**.

## AVERY INVESTIGATES

Stine is the last of the seven confirmed Zodiac victims (five fatalities and two injuries), but others are suspected. Paul Avery, a veteran crime reporter at the *Chronicle*, wrote in 1970[3] that the same killer may have been at work in 1966, too. Avery reported that notes similar to the ones from the Zodiac were sent to the *Riverside Press-Enterprise* and to police after the 1966 slaying of 18-year-old Cheri Jo Bates. Cheri had been lured from her stalled car into a deserted parking lot, where she was stabbed to death. The notes sent afterward said: "Bates had to die there will be more." Avery reported that two of the notes were signed with a "Z".

Paul Avery also connected the Zodiac to the kidnapping of a 23-year-old mother. Kathleen Johns was driving with her 1-year-old daughter from San Bernardino to the San Francisco area when another car flashed its lights at her, prompting her to pull over. A man approached and warned her that one of her car wheels was wobbling and fixed it for her. Kathleen started driving again – only to have that same tyre completely come off the car. The man who had "helped" her stopped again and offered to take her to a gas station. Kathleen agreed, but got a sinking feeling when the man passed by one gas station after another. When she questioned him, he told her he planned to kill her. Kathleen managed to bolt from the car with her daughter and hide in a ditch. When she finally reached a police station to report the indicident, she spotted a Wanted poster featuring a picture of the Zodiac and screamed: "Oh, my god! That's him!"

Another suspected – but unconfirmed – Zodiac case centres on 25-year-old Donna Lass, who disappeared from South Lake Tahoe in September 1970. Six months later, Avery received a postcard he believed was from the Zodiac. The message consisted of cut and pasted newspaper clippings and seemed to say that Lass's body could be found "around in the snow". The note was signed with the cross-and-circle symbol of the Zodiac's past letters. Some thought it could have been a copycat, especially because it came on the heels of another confirmed – and well-publicised – Zodiac communique sent to Avery at the *Chronicle*. Newspapers across the country ran stories about Avery receiving a ghoulish Halloween card in late October 1970. Written neatly in white ink was the message: "Peek-a-boo – you are doomed." It was signed, "From your secret pal". The card was adorned with images of skeletons, as well as a handwritten reference to "paradice slaves" (sic), and the phrase "by fire, by gun and by rope".

Police considered it a threat on Avery's life, but the eccentric reporter declined protection. "I'm really not scared. I've needled him in some of my stories and maybe that's why he wrote to me," he told a reporter, adding: "I do think I'll be a little careful for a while."

The note to Avery was **authenticated** by a handwriting expert who had studied the Zodiac's earlier messages.

## Late January, 1974 / The final confirmed Zodiac letter arrives at the *San Francisco Chronicle*'s office.

In the last of his 18 confirmed letters, the killer praised the classic 1974 horror movie *The Exorcist* as the best satirical comedy he'd ever seen, and claimed his body count had reached 37. After this revelation, the Zodiac Killer seemingly disappeared.

Several supposed Zodiac letters have been deemed **forgeries**.

### THE CARTOONIST'S SUSPECT

The abrupt end to the Zodiac's killing spree only fuelled his mystique. Theories about the killer's true identity are never-ending. Many have stepped forward, claiming to have solved the mystery.

Robert Graysmith, a cartoonist working at the *Chronicle* when the Zodiac Killer announced himself, became obsessed with the case. Graysmith wrote two bestselling books[4] that posited that the killer was Arthur Leigh Allen. Allen – who died in 1992 – had been less-than-honourably discharged from the US Navy in 1958 and fired from a teaching job for molesting a student in 1968. Allen wore a Zodiac-brand watch – the logo of which was similar to the crosshairs signature the killer favoured. In 1974 – the same year that the final Zodiac letter was sent – Allen was arrested for molesting a 12-year-old boy. He pleaded guilty to the charge and served a two-year prison sentence. In 1991, he was also identified in a photo lineup by Michael Mageau, one of the Zodiac Killer's survivors.

Allen was reported to the police by his friend, **Don Cheney**, who became concerned when Allen began talking about wanting to kill people.

In 2007, when a film adaptation of Graysmith's book hit cinemas and interest was renewed in the cold case, detective George Bawart said that he was 95 percent sure Allen was the killer. "What really bothers me about this case is that we were ready to charge Arthur Leigh Allen … but he died before we could do that."[5]

*Zodiac,* the 2007 movie adaptation of Robert Graysmith's book, was directed by David Fincher. Graysmith was played by Jake Gyllenhaal.

## LINGERING DOUBTS

In 2014, a man named Gary Stewart wrote a book, *The Most Dangerous Animal of All*,[6] claiming his biological father was the elusive Zodiac Killer. Stewart had been abandoned in a stairwell as a newborn, and as an adult, he learned that his father was Earl Van Best Jr., a book salesman who Stewart said had disturbing fixations and rage issues. Stewart pointed to his father's appearance – a dead ringer for the police sketch circulated in 1969 – and said that he found his father's initials – EV, Best, and Jr – in a Zodiac cipher sent to the *San Francisco Examiner*. San Francisco police commented that they were investigating the claim.

Several other men – all now dead – also have been tied to the case. One was Louis Myers, whose friend said that before his death in 2002, he had confessed to being the Zodiac Killer, supposedly targeting couples after breaking up with his girlfriend. Myers had connections with several of the victims, attending the same high schools as David Faraday and Betty Lou Jensen, and allegedly working in the same restaurant as Darlene Ferrin. Furthermore, no Zodiac letters were received for a period between 1971 and 1973 – the same time that Myers was stationed overseas with the military.

A suspect named Ross Sullivan had been hospitalised for bipolar disorder and schizophrenia several times. He also wore boots whose soles were similar to the footprints found at Lake Berryessa.

Another suspect with a connection to the Lake Berryessa stabbings was Donald Lee Bujok. He was a felon who was released from a Montana prison in 1968 after serving 11 years for killing a sheriff's deputy. Cecilia Shepard and Bryan Hartnell's attacker told them that he had just escaped a Colorado prison.

Police are still hoping to finally solve the aging case with modern technology. In 2018, Vallejo detectives sent two envelopes containing Zodiac letters to a lab in the hope that saliva from the envelope flap and stamps might contain the killer's DNA. Detective Terry Poyser said if the lab could create a genetic profile based on that DNA, investigators might be able to track down the killer through genealogy websites. "It really comes down to DNA," Poyser said. "Without it, you have nothing."[7]

An expert matched the **handwriting** in the Zodiac Killer's letters to Earl Van Best's signature on his marriage certificate.

A suspect named **Lawrence Kane** had allegedly pestered Darlene at her work.

# STRANGER DANGER

**Like any loving parents, those in Oakland County, Michigan, often told their children to stay away from strangers. These routine, everyday warnings were suddenly justified in the cruelest way possible.**

The case of the so-called Oakland County Child Killer, named after the Michigan county in which four terrifying kidnappings and murders occurred, panicked parents throughout the Midwest. The details were baffling. The two male victims bore signs of sexual assault, but the two females did not. Three were suffocated or strangled, while one died of a shotgun blast to the head. All appeared to have been bathed at some point and were discovered neatly dressed.

## THE FIRST VICTIM

Twelve-year-old Mark Stebbins and his older brother Mike regularly hung out together at an American Legion Hall at 9 Mile and Woodward, about a mile from their home in Ferndale, Michigan. The veterans' organization was a safe place for the boys to spend time, and on a snowy Sunday in February 1976, they walked to the hall to play pool.

After a while, Mark – described as a good student who liked to spend time alone – said he wanted to walk home to watch television. It was a path he had taken countless times before, both with his brother and by himself. But on this day, Mark did not arrive home, and his mother,

*Opposite page, clockwise from top:* The body of Kristine Mihelich is removed from a snowbank in Franklin Village; Timothy King; Kristine Mihelich; Mark Stebbins; Jill Robinson; artist sketch of the killer; an artist's sketch of the killer; suspect Theodore Lamborgine.

4 VICTIMS | 5 KEY SUSPECTS

Ruth, called police in a panic. While Mark Stebbins' disappearance worried those who knew him, it was not the type of case that would normally receive widespread media attention. That changed four days later, when an office worker in the nearby town of Southfield spotted his body, abandoned in a parking lot.

# 19 February 1976 / Mark Stebbins' body is found.

Mark had rope burns on his wrists, but he was not bound, and it appeared that he had been strangled or suffocated at least a day earlier. Ferndale Police Chief Donald Geary told reporters the boy's body likely had been kept in the trunk of a car before being ditched in the parking lot. Not only had he been scrubbed clean, but his fingernails had been scraped by his killer. As the police investigated and Mark's family mourned, months passed by and the tragic case slipped quietly from the headlines.

## CONNECTED KILLINGS

On December 26, 1976, a motorist found the body of 12-year-old Jill Robinson in Troy, Michigan. She had left her Royal Oak home four days earlier after a row with her mother over what to have for dinner. On the surface, it was tough to discern if Jill's death was related to Mark's. The little girl had died in a completely different manner – a shotgun blast to the head rather than asphyxiation. But a few striking similarities led police to believe that there must be a connection: Jill's parents were also divorced; like Mark, she was described as a loner; and it appeared she had been kidnapped and held for days before being killed. As with Mark, she had been fed and given water to drink while held captive. Her body, like Mark's, was dumped on a day it had snowed, helping to obscure much-needed evidence.

The killer's pace quickened. The next victim disappeared just a week later, on 2 January 1977, after leaving a party shop just four blocks from her house in nearby Berkley, Michigan. Ten-year-old Kristine Mihelich had bought a magazine and was walking along a busy

The killer targeted mostly **affluent areas** of the southern portion of the county.

It is possible that Jill was killed with a **shotgun** when strangulation didn't work.

The search for Kristine included **helicopter sweeps**.

thoroughfare in broad daylight when she vanished. Because Jill's body had been found so recently, Kristine's disappearance was treated with far more urgency. Officers canvassed the neighbourhood looking for witnesses and clues but found nothing. A week after Kristine vanished, police assumed the worst – and that scared them.[1]

# "IF SOMEONE CAN BE SNATCHED OFF A BUSY STREET AT 3:00 P.M. ON A SUNDAY AFTERNOON, HOW CAN YOU PROTECT ANYONE?"

SGT. DAVID PICHE

The *Detroit News* offered a reward of **$100,000** to catch the killer.

These fears were realised when snow fell on 22 January 1977 – 19 days after Kristine's disappearance. Mail carrier Jerry Wozny discovered Kristine's body in a ditch along a dead-end road in Franklin, Michigan, another Oakland County town. "I saw a hand. It scared the hell out of me," Wozny told reporters. He said it appeared that snow had been tossed on top of her body to make her difficult to spot.[2] The headlines the next day read: SLAYINGS TERRORIZE COUNTY.[3]

## THE FINAL DISAPPEARANCE

**A blue AMC Gremlin** was seen parked in the lot where Tim King was last seen. In 2013, parts of a similar car were found buried in a field in Grand Blanc, Michigan.

Less than two months later, that terror reached the King family. On 16 March 1977, 11-year-old Tim asked his sister Kathy for 30 cents so he could buy candy from a drugstore three blocks from home. He left his house in Birmingham, Michigan, at about 8:15 p.m. and skateboarded to the Hunter-Maple Pharmacy. The shop assistant, Amy Walters, saw him leave with his candy at about 8:30 p.m. through a rear door that led to a darkened parking lot. Tim never returned home.

Tim's parents insisted that they had **warned** their son repeatedly to never talk to strangers.

Tim King's body was found a week later. Like the other victims, he had been kept alive much of the time he had been missing. Officials believed that he was suffocated within an hour of being found. While Tim was missing, his mother had written a letter to the *Detroit News*, pleading for him to come home for some Kentucky Fried Chicken, his favourite meal. An autopsy of the body revealed the food that he had eaten just before he was killed – fried chicken.

Tim's meticulously clean body was found in a ditch along a well-travelled dirt road in Livonia, Michigan, with his skateboard placed next to it. The location marked a change in pattern, as Livonia fell in Wayne County, rather than neighbouring Oakland. Police and sheriff's deputies from both jurisdictions were therefore dedicated to the case.

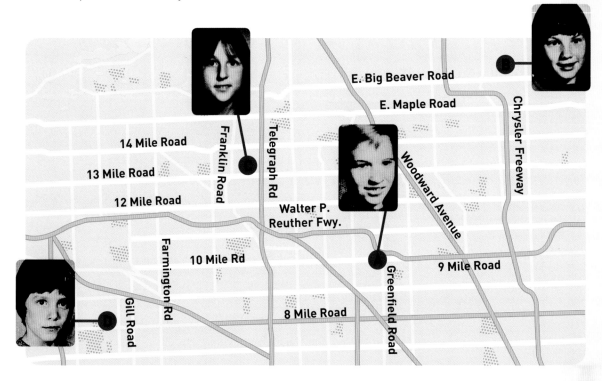

## LOCATIONS OF THE BODIES

- Mark Stebbins: 19 February 1976
- Jill Robinson: 26 December 1976
- Kristine Mihelich: 22 January 1977
- Timothy King: 22 March 1977

### Oakland County, Michigan

- Area: 2,349 km² (907 sq. miles)
- 1976 population: 962,611

## POLICE DESCRIPTIONS

All four victims had white **dog hair** on their otherwise clean bodies.

**Two other abductions** were linked to the case: Cynthia Cadieux, 16, battered to death; and Jane Allen, 14, killed by carbon monoxide. poisoning.

Enough witnesses finally came forward for the police to create a sketch of a suspect. The face that emerged belonged to a white man with dark hair, a prominent nose and thick lips. Bushy muttonchops ran down his cheeks. An accompanying psychological profile told the community they were looking for someone from 20 to 35 years old, who was well-educated and worked in a white-collar job with enough flexibility to give him the freedom to carry out his terrible crimes. "We believe that he appears sane 99 percent of the time," said Birmingham Police Chief Jerry Tobin, who suggested that the killer might be seeing a psychiatrist. Tobin urged anyone in the medical or legal professions to come forward with any information.[4] The police also began to suspect that the killer was being protected by someone close to him – a relative or a friend.

# "NO INDIVIDUAL COULD HAVE KEPT FOUR CHILDREN FOR VARYING LENGTHS OF TIME WITHOUT SOMEONE KNOWING."

BIRMINGHAM POLICE CHIEF JERRY TOBIN

The Kings' request that officials be forced to release more evidence was **denied** by the Michigan Supreme Court in 2017.

It was probably because of that suspicion that family members of the victims were stonewalled by investigators. This was very frustrating to Tim's parents, who had been especially cooperative in humouring investigators' hunches early on. Detectives had believed that whoever was holding Tim hostage would react badly to his parents' emotional pleas, so the couple had agreed to conceal their grief and keep their tone positive during news conferences. The Kings felt that they had received little cooperation from the authorities in return and subsequently sued the county prosecutor's office, hoping to force it to release more evidence from the case. In 2012, the office did release 6,000 pages of case documents.

## SUSPECT SPECULATION

Little official information meant that over the years, rumours have abounded over the identity of the Oakland County Child Killer. Was he a mysterious man named "John", or a priest or someone posing as a police officer? Few actual names were publicly tied to the case. Among the first was David Norberg, an autoworker who drove a car that looked similar to one described near Tim's abduction site. Norberg had been suspected of killing two girls in the late 1970s, though he was not convicted. After he died in a car crash in 1981, his wife found a small silver cross inscribed with the name "Kristine" She remembered the girl who had been the Oakland County Child Killer's third victim and showed the cross to Kristine's aunt, who said it was identical to one Kristine had worn at the Romeo Peach Festival shortly before her death.

Police exhumed Norberg's body in 1999 to see if his DNA matched evidence from the case, but the results did not tie him to the murders. Some investigators say that there is no way that Norberg – a heavy drinker – would have been able to lure stranger-danger-conscious children into his car, and he has largely been dismissed as a suspect.

A convicted paedophile named Christopher Busch was on the shortlist for the King family and Erica McAvoy – Kristine's half-sister. The son of a wealthy auto executive, Busch lived in the area at the time. He was questioned soon after Tim's death and he admitted to investigators that he was a paedophile. He also drove a car that looked similar to one spotted at one of the abductions. Investigators wanted to keep him in jail, but L. Brooks Patterson – who headed the prosecutor's office during the killings – released him as part of a plea deal. In November 1978, just a few months later, Busch killed himself in his home. A drawing of a screaming boy that resembled Mark Stebbins was reportedly found pinned to the wall.

## DNA LINKS

Another suspect is James Gunnels, a 56-year-old man connected to Kristine's murder through DNA evidence. In 2012, investigators

A side-effect of the investigation was the **exposure** of a child pornography ring based on North Fox Island, Lake Michigan.

The **special task force** assigned to the case disbanded in December 1978.

Police received more than **18,000** clues to the killer from the public.

DNA tests in 2013 quashed allegations that notorious serial killer of teenage boys **John Wayne Gacy** was the murderer.

revealed that a strand of hair found on Kristine was a mitochondrial match for Gunnels – meaning that it could have come from him or someone on his mother's side of the family. Gunnels was no more than 16 when the crimes were committed, and he had been raped by Busch. In 2012, Gunnels met with the King family and insisted he knew nothing of the crimes.

In 2012, another tenuous DNA test produced a suspect named Arch Sloan, who was serving a life sentence for the rape of a 10-year-old boy in 1983. A hair found in his 1966 Pontiac Bonneville matched hair found at both Mark and Tim's crime scenes. Although the hair was not Sloan's, investigators believed it belonged to an acquaintance of his.

## THE SEARCH FOR JUSTICE

While the King and Mihelich families zeroed in on Busch as a suspect, Mark Stebbins' family filed a wrongful death lawsuit in 2007 against Theodore Lamborgine, a man who, like Sloan, was in prison for life on assault convictions. David A. Binkley, a lawyer representing the Stebbins family, said that his clients did not think Lamborgine acted alone and hoped the suit would help to uncover more information. He pointed to Lamborgine's refusal to take a polygraph test despite being offered a massively reduced prison sentence if he answered questions about the Oakland County child killings. "Wouldn't you deny being the Oakland County Child Killer?" Binkley said.[5] Despite the family's suspicions, the suit was dismissed in 2008, but the presiding judge left room for it to be refiled if more evidence should come to light.

Tim's father, Barry King, has replayed time and again how he had talked to his son after the community learned of Kristine's death. "All my kids remember me telling Tim, 'If anyone tries to pick you up, drop everything and run and scream,'" he said. "Part of the tragedy to me is, once Tim got into the car, he knew what would happen. That's the worst part of it all."[6] As long as the mystery of the Oakland County Child Killer remains unsolved, the Kings and the other victims' families will remain haunted by the events of over 40 years ago, still searching for answers that always seem just out of reach.

Sloan was convicted of first-degree **criminal sexual conduct** – the legal term used in Michigan for rape, sexual assault, or sexual battery.

In 2012, an unidentified investigator known as "Bob" claimed that there were between 11 and 16 victims, and that the killings were connected to **Satanic rituals.** These claims were dismissed due to lack of evidence.

In 2013, the King family produced a documentary titled **Decades of Deceit** detailing what they perceived as the bungled investigation into their son's murder.

# DEATH AT THE DRUGSTORE

**Tylenol is one of the US's leading over-the-counter remedies for pain and fever. However, in September 1982, after taking the harmless drug, people in Chicago started dropping down dead.**

Mary Kellerman woke up one Wednesday morning in 1982 feeling a bit under the weather. Her parents did what many do when hearing sore-throat complaints: they gave her Extra-Strength Tylenol to ease the pain before it was time for her to head off to school in the Chicago suburb of Elk Grove Village, Illinois. Mary padded into the bathroom and closed the door. Her father heard a sudden, loud thump. Paramedics tried to save Mary, but nothing helped. The twelve-year-old girl was pronounced dead by 10 a.m.

Across town, a 27-year-old postal worker named Adam Janus woke up sick enough to call off work. He picked up his kids from morning preschool and stopped by a pharmacy in another Chicago suburb to get some medicine. He fixed his children lunch, then prescribed himself two Tylenol and a nap. Minutes later, he collapsed in his kitchen. Medics suspected a heart attack, despite his young age and seemingly good health. No one could have known that Mary and Adam's deaths were tragically linked, despite the two having never met. They would be the first of seven victims killed by Extra-Strength Tylenol capsules poisoned with potassium cyanide.

*Opposite page, clockwise from top:* Jack Eliason and his wife Nancy hold up a picture, taken in 1974, of Jack's sister Mary McFarland (on right), poisoned by the Tylenol killer; James W. Lewis and Roger Arnold, two of the suspects; as alarm spreads, a drugstore clerk in New York City removes Tylenol from the shelves.

EXTRA-STRENGTH
TYLENOL

CAPSULES

no aspirin

A-
NGTH
LENOL

STRENGTH
NOL
MEDICATION

7 VICTIMS | 5 DRUGSTORES | 3 KEY SUSPECTS

Devastated family members gathered in mourning at Adam Janus' home. The dead man's younger brother, 25-year-old Stanley, felt chronic back pain flaring up, and Stanley's 19-year-old wife Theresa had a headache, brought on by the stress of the heartbreaking day. The couple both swallowed some Tylenol from Adam's cupboard. Stanley collapsed first, then Theresa.

Thomas Kim, medical director of the Northwest Community Hospital's intensive care unit, had been the one to sign Adam's paperwork indicating that he had suffered a heart attack. He was about to leave for home when he heard that more members of the Janus family were being rushed to his unit. Kim later told reporters of his shock at these sudden developments. He had met Stanley just hours earlier. "I had been talking to this six-foot, healthy guy," he said.[1] When he learned Stanley's wife was also dangerously ill, he knew he was dealing with something far more sinister than a heart attack.

The same day that Mary Kellerman and Adam Janus died – 29 September 1982 – a woman named Mary "Lynn" Reiner suffered the same fate. At 3:45 p.m., the broad-smiled 27-year-old, who had given birth just days earlier, popped some Tylenol for her pain. She collapsed and died soon after.

As investigators searched the Janus house, another woman – 31-year-old Mary McFarland – told her coworkers at an Illinois Bell shop in Lombard that she had a headache and went into a back room to take some Tylenol. She collapsed within minutes, and died.

## MAKING CONNECTIONS

In hindsight, it is easy to see Tylenol as a common thread. However, for investigators at the time, the use of this over-the-counter medication was so mundane that it did not jump out as the cause of death. What Dr Kim did soon figure out was that the victims all showed symptoms of potassium cyanide poisoning – abdominal pain, dizziness and heart failure. Blood tests confirmed his diagnosis and, as he later told reporters, he paced his office, trying to work out how these disparate people had all been exposed to the same toxin.

By the end of Wednesday, barely 12 hours after little Mary Kellerman was pronounced dead, two suburban firefighters who had been monitoring chatter on the fire radios they kept in their homes started comparing notes on the phone. The firefighters shared their theory with Kim, who knew the Januses had taken Tylenol but hadn't known about the other victims. Authorities retrieved the red-and-white bottles from all of the victims' homes and realised they came from the same lot and shared expiration dates.[2]

# "I SAID, 'THIS IS A WILD STAB, BUT MAYBE IT'S TYLENOL'."
## FIREFIGHTER RICHARD KEYWORTH

Nicholas Pishos, an investigator for the Cook County medical examiner's office, had studied cyanide in a college biology class. He and chief medical examiner Edmund Donoghue were discussing the murders over the phone when Donoghue remembered that cyanide has a distinctive smell. Pishos opened the bottles. "I said, 'Whoops. I smell something. It smells like almonds,'" he later told a reporter.[3]

Lab tests confirmed that whoever was behind the tampering had made it a gunless game of Russian roulette. In each bottle, a handful of the capsules had been emptied and replaced with a lethal dose of cyanide. Between 5 and 7 micrograms of cyanide is fatal, and the contaminated capsules contained as much as 65 milligrams of the poison – several thousand times more than a fatal dose. The people who consumed these capsules typically collapsed within minutes.

Taking **cyanide** causes heart muscle cells and nerve cells to be robbed of oxygen. Muscles seize up, bodies convulse and contract, and the heartbeat weakens until it stops completely.

## PANIC IN CHICAGO

By Thursday, just one day after the first deaths, the media were warning all of Chicago – and soon the country – about the Tylenol connection. Chicago police, worried residents might miss the news, went through the streets broadcasting the message over loudspeakers. Investigators with the US Food and Drug Administration warned consumers to avoid buying Tylenol and not to take any already in their homes. Pharmacy owners pulled the drug from their shelves, and Johnson & Johnson – the parent firm for Tylenol maker McNeil Consumer Products Co. – offered refunds to panicked customers.

## POISONED PILLS

McNeil officials ruled out tampering during production. The company routinely kept a random sample of pills from every lot produced. They tested the lot in question – MC2880, expiration date April 1987 – after the deaths. "They were clean," said McNeil spokeswoman Elsie Bemer. This finding led authorities to believe that someone in Chicago had bought the Tylenol bottles legitimately, taken them home, tampered with the capsules and then put them back on shelves throughout the city. Unwitting customers bought them, never knowing when they paid for their simple bottle of headache medicine that they were sealing their – or their loved ones' – fate.

Meanwhile, the body count grew. On Friday, 1 October, 35-year-old Paula Prince was found in her Chicago apartment. She had last been seen at a Walgreens on North Wells Street on Wednesday, just after the flight attendant had landed in O'Hare from Las Vegas. Surveillance photos showed Prince buying a bottle of Tylenol at about 9:30 p.m. that night. She had no way of knowing that across town, doctors were on the cusp of tying tainted Tylenol capsules to a spate of sudden deaths.

# 30 September 1982 / The final victim, Paula Prince, dies after taking Tylenol.

Prince died soon after taking the pills, but her body was not discovered for two days. "Her sister was supposed to meet her for dinner, and [Paula] wasn't answering her telephone," friend and fellow flight attendant Joan Ahern later commented.[3] According to Richard Brzeczek, superintendent of the Chicago Police Department, Paula Prince had gone to the bathroom to remove her makeup and popped the meds while in there. "The Tylenol bottle was still sitting open on the vanity," Brzeczek commented. "She took it in the bathroom, and by the time she got to the threshold of the door, she was dead."

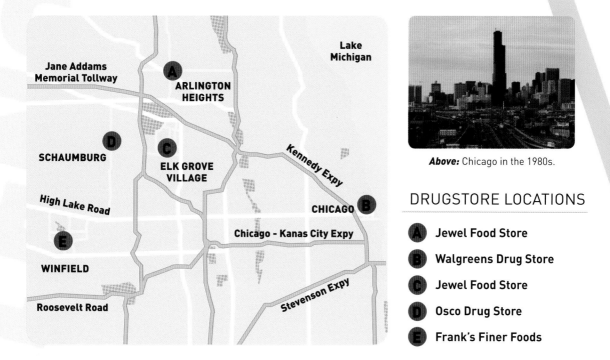

*Above:* Chicago in the 1980s.

## DRUGSTORE LOCATIONS

A Jewel Food Store

B Walgreens Drug Store

C Jewel Food Store

D Osco Drug Store

E Frank's Finer Foods

## DEAD ENDS

As panicked as Chicago was, the rest of the nation could take comfort in knowing that the attack appeared to be isolated – until it didn't. A few days into the high-profile investigation, news spread that other victims were falling ill nationwide from various poisons, including rat poison and hydrochloric acid. Authorities investigated and found that these incidents were caused by opportunistic copycats. It seemed that anyone with a grudge was jumping aboard the pill-tainting bandwagon. Some even branched out to new methods, hiding sharp pins in Halloween candy, leading some communities to ban trick-or-treating altogether.

As soon as the method and means were pinpointed in the Tylenol poisonings case, the police expressed confidence that the perpetrator would be swiftly apprehended. But that didn't happen. Five days after the deaths began – when the tally had reached seven – Illinois Attorney

**Newspaper headlines** warned: CYANIDE DEADLY JUST TO TOUCH.

The Food and Drug Administration (FDA) tallied more than **270** different incidents of copycat tampering.

General Tyrone Fahner announced that the police were searching for a man who had been arrested in August for shoplifting Tylenol. It seemed a promising lead on the surface, but Fahner tempered public expectations: "We're not quite sure what to think. Sometimes people steal anything. They may have just been stealing Tylenol to steal it."[4] The shoplifter story made big headlines but was quickly discounted. It turned out that he'd been behind bars since his August arrest. He was just one of several fruitless leads pursued.

Investigators also sought to interview disgruntled employees with both Johnson & Johnson and McNeil. They took notes on tips about suspicious-looking customers. One pharmacy employee was arrested after police got a tip he kept cyanide in his house. The man was eventually cleared after the supposed cyanide turned out to be a nontoxic cleaning agent.

Investigators weighed theories that there was more than one capsule-tamperer – a hypothesis posited because some of the capsules had clearly been modified, while the spiking of others was far better disguised. The nation's top sleuths came up empty-handed.

## INNOCENT VICTIM

One of the more promising early suspects was a man named Roger Arnold, who had worked alongside the father of one of the victims in a Jewel Food Stores warehouse. Arnold, then 48, was arrested in October 1982 after a tip-off that he had cyanide in his home. Police interrogated Arnold for three days, after which they dismissed any link between him and the Tylenol deaths. Arnold considered his life ruined, however, and wanted revenge against the secret informant. In January 1983, he targeted a Chicago man he believed had directed investigators his way. Arnold shot and killed John Stanisha – a 46-year-old computer consultant and father of three who police say was never an informant. Arnold lamented the death years later. "I killed a man, a perfectly innocent person," he said from prison in 1996. "I had choices. I could have walked away."[5]

The most likely break in the case came courtesy of a brazen

More than **100 investigators,** including those who had helped build cases against the serial killers Richard Speck and John Wayne Gacy, joined forces to solve the mystery.

John Stanisha has been referred to as the **eighth** Tylenol victim.

Arnold served **14 years** of a 30-year prison sentence and died in 2008.

extortionist. Within two weeks of the deadly outbreak, Tylenol's makers, Johnson & Johnson, received a letter promising to stop the killings for $1 million. The letter, immediately given to the FBI, was traced to James W. Lewis of New York City.

Lewis' letter was dismissed as heartless opportunism, but he still routinely appears as the frontrunner on lists of suspects – largely because no one else has emerged to unseat him. There are certain suspicious factors. At one point in his checkered past, Lewis and his wife LeAnn had imported pill-making machines from India; and when he and his wife had first moved to Chicago, they had lived under false names as Robert and Nancy Richardson. Additionally, Lewis had once been charged with bludgeoning and dismembering a Kansas City man. Those charges were dismissed after a judge ruled that Lewis' arrest and the seizure of his property were illegal. As recently as 2009, federal authorities searched Lewis' home hoping to discover new clues. Nothing was found.

Two years later, the FBI took a DNA sample from Ted Kaczynski, the man famously dubbed the Unabomber for mailing 16 homemade bombs that killed three people and injured more than 20 between 1978 and 1995. Imprisoned since 1996, Kaczynski was on the police's radar because he had lived with his parents in suburban Chicago during the Tylenol murders. Every lead led to big headlines, but nothing more.

## SAFETY FIRST

The only solid progress ever made in the case involved packaging. Within days of the deaths, legislators proposed new laws requiring manufacturers to seal drug containers. The little foil seals are commonplace now, but prior to young Mary Kellerman collapsing in her bathroom, all that stood between a malevolent would-be tamperer and a stranger's medicine was a twist-off lid and a wad of cotton.

Pishos, one of the original investigators, recently lamented that the killer remains nameless after all these years. "It's frustrating for everybody," he said, "more so for the families who were victims not being able to put this person or persons behind bars."[6]

---

Lewis did not ask for the **$1 million** to be paid to himself, but into the account of a businessman whom he claimed had swindled him and his wife.

Lewis served 12 years for **extortion** but has never been directly tied to the Tylenol deaths.

In 2010, **James Lewis** published a novel titled *Poison! The Doctor's Dilemma*. It was about people dying after unknowingly drinking poisoned water.

# A CHRISTMAS NIGHTMARE

**A missing beauty queen, a bizarre ransom note and a body in the basement. The tragic death of young JonBenét Ramsey was a multifaceted enigma that would defy explanation.**

Six-year-old beauty queen JonBenét Ramsey was destined for stardom. John and Patsy, her parents, were convinced of it. A former Miss West Virginia herself, Patsy Ramsey was determined that her pretty daughter should follow in her glamorous footsteps. In a cruel twist of fate, JonBenét would be buried in the same sparkly dress that she competed in. The tragic details of her death – and the mysterious circumstances surrounding it – make it one of America's most notorious unsolved child murder cases.

## AN IDEAL HOME

From a very young age, JonBenét was entered into beauty pageants. Dressed in flashy outfits embellished with sequins or other eye-catching decoration, she would stand centre stage and perform her well-practiced routine. The Sunburst National Pageant, Little Miss Colorado, Little Miss Charlevoix, Colorado State All-Star Kids Cover Girl and America's Royale Miss – JonBenét had competed in all of these beauty pageants and in many cases, won them. Just two weeks before she was brutally slain, she had been crowned "Little Miss Christmas".

*Opposite page, main image:* JonBenét Ramsey.
*Opposite page, clockwise from top:* The Ramsey family home; John and Patsy Ramsey appeal for information about their daughter's murder; JonBenét Ramsey in one of her beauty pageant costumes; suspect John Mark Karr.

**1 VICTIM**

The world remembers JonBenét with bleach-blonde hair and a face full of makeup, but there was much more to this bright little girl. She excelled in mathematics and was fascinated by nature. She enjoyed following around the Ramseys' gardener, Brian Scott, while he worked.[1]

# "I REMEMBER HOW INTELLIGENT JONBENÉT WAS. THAT'S WHY I NEVER TALKED TO HER AS IF SHE WERE JUST A LITTLE KID."

BRIAN SCOTT

## AN IDEAL HOME

The Ramsey family – 6-year-old JonBenét, her 9-year-old brother Burke, and John and Patsy – lived at 755 15th Street, Boulder, Colorado. Their home was an impressive brick house in the Tudor Revival style on a tree-lined avenue.

John Ramsey was President of Access Graphics, a successful computer company, while Patsy was a former pageant star turned housewife. The Ramsey family seemed to epitomise the American dream: a beautiful family, an exquisite house and a vacation home in picturesque Charlevoix, Michigan. As Christmas 1996 approached, the Ramseys sent out their usual greeting card detailing the things the family had done during the year, along with a festive photograph. This was the last card they would send as a family of four.

On Christmas evening, the Ramsey family went to their old friends Fleet and Priscilla White's party, which they attended every year. The family left around 10 p.m. Since they were traveling to their vacation home in Charlevoix the next morning and wanted to make an early start, according to John and Patsy, the whole family went straight to bed. Packing for the trip could wait until the morning. At around 5:45 a.m., Patsy Ramsey awoke and discovered a three-page, handwritten note on the spiral staircase that led from the master bedroom to the kitchen:

In December 1994, **2,000** people visited the Ramsey's home for a guided tour organised by The Boulder Historical Society.

John Ramsey had three children from a previous marriage. In 1992, his eldest daughter, Elizabeth, died in a **car crash** aged 22.

132

Mr. Ramsey,

Listen carefully! We are a group of individuals that represent a small foreign faction. We do respect your bussiness [sic] but not the country that it serves. At this time we have your daughter in our posession [sic]. She is safe and unharmed and if you want her to see 1997, you must follow our instructions to the letter.

You will withdraw $118,000.00 from your account. $100,000 will be in $100 bills and the remaining $18,000 in $20 bills. Make sure that you bring an adequate size attache to the bank. When you get home you will put the money in a brown paper bag. I will call you between 8 and 10 am tomorrow to instruct you on delivery. The delivery will be exhausting so I advise you to be rested. If we monitor you getting the money early, we might call you early to arrange an earlier delivery of the money and hence a earlier ~~delivery~~ pick-up of your daughter.

Any deviation of my instructions will result in the immediate execution of your daughter. You will also be denied her remains for proper burial. The two gentlemen watching over your daughter do not particularly like you so I advise you not to provoke them. Speaking to anyone about your situation, such as Police, F.B.I., etc., will result in your daughter being beheaded. If we catch you talking to a stray dog, she dies. If you alert bank authorities, she dies. If the money is in any way marked or tampered with, she dies. You will be scanned for electronic devices and if any are found, she dies. You can try to deceive us but be warned that we are familiar with law enforcement countermeasures and tactics. You stand a 99% chance of killing your daughter if you try to out smart us. Follow our instructions and you stand a 100% chance of getting her back.

You and your family are under constant scrutiny as well as the authorities. Don't try to grow a brain John. You are not the only fat cat around so don't think that killing will be difficult. Don't underestimate us John. Use that good southern common sense of yours. It is up to you now John!

Victory!
S.B.T.C

The length of the **ransom note** was highly unusual.

**Experts** have claimed that the note could have been written after the murder.

**73** suspects' handwriting was analyzed to discover who could have written the note.

No one knows what the initials **S.B.T.C.** stand for.

## THE RAMSEY HOME

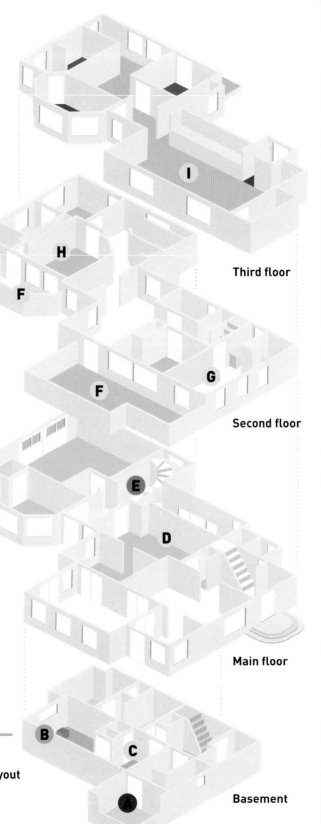

**A** JonBenét's body

**B** Broken window and suitcase

**C** Toy train room

**D** Kitchen

**E** Ransom note and writing pads

**F** Balcony

**G** Burke's bedroom

**H** JonBenét's bedroom

**I** John and Patsy's bedroom

Third floor

Second floor

Main floor

Basement

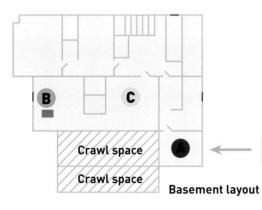

Crawl space

Crawl space

**Basement layout**

After reading the note, Patsy rushed upstairs to find that JonBenét wasn't asleep where she should be. She wasn't in her bedroom. She wasn't in the bathroom. She was gone. Disregarding the conditions laid down in the threatening note, Patsy called 911. She then called several friends, including Fleet and Priscilla White, and begged them to come over immediately for moral support.[2]

# "WE HAVE A KIDNAPPING. HURRY, PLEASE."

## PATSY RAMSEY TO 911 OPERATOR KIM ARCHULETA

Several people were even reported to have **cleaned** the house as they attempted to keep themselves busy while waiting for news.

The first officer on the scene, Rick French, was unable to find any sign of forced entry and noted that the house's security system had not been activated the night before. Contrary to normal protocol, the house was not cordoned off to preserve potential evidence. Police officers, the Ramseys and their friends roamed freely around the place. At the designated time for the kidnapper to call, no phone call came.

### THE WHITE DOOR

A **suitcase** had been placed below a broken basement window.

Marks on JonBenét's face could have been made by a **stun gun** or a piece of electric train track that belonged to Burke.

A single, unidentified **footprint** was later found near the body – but none in the snow outside the window.

At approximately 2:00 p.m., an officer told John and Fleet to conduct another search of the house. John took the lead and they headed towards the basement. Near the back was a small white door leading to a wine cellar, which had been ignored during the initial search, as Officer French had only been looking for exit or entry points to the house. Inside this cellar, John and Fleet found JonBenét's lifeless body. She was lying on her back with her arms raised above her head. A blanket was over her body and her mouth was sealed shut with duct tape. White cord was looped around her wrist and neck. Attached to the cord was a makeshift garrote constructed from a piece of a paintbrush. She had also received a blow to the head. As soon as he saw his daughter, John ripped the tape from her mouth, scooped her up in his arms and rushed upstairs to the living room. Unfortunately, this act would prove extremely harmful to the investigation – the body should not have been touched, let alone moved, until a medical examiner had arrived on the scene. At this stage, the crime scene was severely compromised.

An autopsy concluded that JonBenét had been asphyxiated; she had also suffered blunt force trauma to the head, leading to craniocerebral trauma. Although there was no evidence of conventional rape, sexual assault could not be ruled out. Undigested pineapple was found in her stomach, indicating that she had eaten the fruit within two hours of her death. Further investigation revealed the other half of the paintbrush among Patsy's art supplies in the basement.

## A FAMILY AFFAIR

On the kitchen table, investigators found a bowl of half-eaten pineapple, as well as a heavy flashlight, though this was not thought important. The ransom note had been written using a pen and notepad that came from the kitchen. A rough draft of the note was also discovered. Whoever wrote it must have had detailed knowledge of the family's life. Moreover, he or she must have been able to move easily around the house in the dark and find the wine cellar in the basement.

In the basement, a small window had been smashed. While this initially seemed suspicious, John said that he had broken it months earlier after accidentally locking himself out. On the windowsill was a layer of undisturbed dust and dirt as well as an intact spider web, suggesting that it was not an entry or exit point for an intruder.

The length and language of the ransom note was highly revealing to some investigators, who felt that the handwriting looked similar to Patsy Ramsey's. The $118,000 figure that was demanded was the exact amount John Ramsey had received as a Christmas bonus, something that very few people could have known. Handwriting experts from the Colorado Bureau of Investigation decided that John Ramsey did not write the note, but their analysis regarding Patsy was inconclusive. Convinced that the police were regarding them as prime suspects in the murder of their daughter, both John and Patsy hired separate lawyers and refused to speak to investigators. They felt that they had told police everything they knew and could provide no more worthwhile insights into the case.

Moving the **body** made it hard for police to determine cause of death.

Patsy said that JonBenét had **not eaten** pineapple that day, and that she had gone straight to bed after the Whites' party.

Both Patsy and Burke Ramsey's **fingerprints** were found on the bowl of pineapple.

The Ramseys hired their own **private investigator**, Ellis Amistead.

The Ramseys offered a **$50,000** reward for any information that could lead to the arrest of the killer.

# 30 April 1997 / John and Patsy Ramsey finally agree to separate formal interviews at the Boulder County Justice.

In March 1997 John Ramsey's two adult children, John Andrew and Melinda, were **cleared** as suspects.

John and Patsy would only agree to an interview on condition that they received the police reports so that they could prepare for the questions. To the police, their reluctance to cooperate seemed to conflict with their earlier statements that they would do whatever was necessary to aid the investigation.

Some analyzed that JonBenét's incontinence was a protest against the **pressure** of the beauty pageants.

Throughout her short life, JonBenét had a frequent tendency to wet the bed. For some, this cast further suspicion on John and Patsy, as bedwetting is often a response in children to abuse. The underwear that JonBenét was wearing when her body was found was stained with urine, and pull-up diapers were hanging out of the closet outside JonBenét's bedroom. A theory circulated that Patsy accidentally killed JonBenét in a fit of rage following a bedwetting accident, causing Patsy to scoff, "Does someone actually think I would kill my child because she wet the bed?"[3]

Linda maintained that the **blanket** JonBenét's body had been wrapped in had most likely come from a clothes dryer near JonBenét's bedroom.

One witness who appeared before a grand jury was Linda Hoffmann-Pugh, the Ramseys' housekeeper at the time of JonBenét's murder. During the investigation, Linda voiced suspicions that Patsy was guilty of her daughter's murder, stating that she argued with her often. "I think she had multiple personalities. She'd be in a good mood and then she'd be cranky," she relayed in her statement.[4]

**Patsy Ramsey** died of ovarian cancer on 24 June 2006, aged 49.

Over the ensuing years, John and Patsy Ramsey remained under a cloud of suspicion. In 1999, the Boulder grand jury voted to indict both parents on two counts each of child abuse resulting in the death of JonBenét. However, the Ramseys were never indicted because the district attorney, Alex Hunter, refused to sign the documents.

## THE BROTHER'S BEHAVIOUR

Following questioning by a grand jury, authorities confirmed that Burke Ramsey – who was just 9 years old at the time of the murder – was not a suspect. However, JonBenét's brother became a favourite culprit among many internet sleuths over the years. His seemingly lighthearted, casual attitude during a taped interview with a child specialist on 8 January – just two weeks after the death of his younger sister – caught the attention of several people. There was speculation that Burke had been violent with JonBenét in the past. According to a family photographer, he had hit her in the head with a golf club a year earlier. In December 2016, Burke's lawyers filed a defamation lawsuit totalling $750 million against CBS for speculating that he was the killer in their television documentary *The Case of: JonBenét Ramsey*.

In 2008, Boulder County DA Mary Lacy exonerated the entire Ramsey family on the basis that their DNA did not match unidentified male DNA found on two items of JonBenét's clothing. However, it transpired that the partial DNA profile that was obtained contained a mixture of DNA – belonging to JonBenét; an unknown male and; in one sample, a third unidentified person.

## OUTSIDERS AND INTRUDERS

Linda Hoffmann-Pugh and her handyman husband, Mervin, were also not safe from suspicion. Patsy told investigators that Linda had money problems and once asked the Ramseys for a loan. Moreover, Linda had a key to the house and was familiar with its layout. It was speculated that if JonBenét had been killed by an intruder or intruders, they could have had a key, since there was no obvious sign of forced entry. However, Linda and Mervin were never formally accused of the crime.

At the time of JonBenét's murder, Gary Oliva – a drifter with a history of sexually abusing minors – lived just a few blocks away from the Ramsey home. When he was picked up on an unrelated charge four years later, police found a photograph of JonBenét and a stun gun in his backpack. A search of his apartment revealed an eerie shrine to JonBenét. Police took Oliva to the station to question him about the murder. He was grilled for hours, asked to provide DNA and writing samples, then released without charge. Someone who was convinced of Oliva's guilt was his own high school friend, Michael Vail, who claimed that just after JonBenét's murder, Oliva called him in a panic and said that he had "hurt a little girl", before hanging up.[5] In 2018, it was reported

Former friends and neighbours of the Ramseys stated that Burke had a **temper** and was jealous of the attention that his sister received.

In a 2016 TV interview, **Burke Ramsey** said that the murderer was "some paedophile in the pageant audience".

A sample of **male DNA** on JonBenét's underwear could have potentially been transferred during the manufacturing process.

It is possible that Linda would have known how much money John had been given as a Christmas **bonus.**

Oliva claimed he "never lusted over" his JonBenét **shrine**, but instead "would look at the pictures and cry."

Gary Oliva is currently serving a **prison sentence** for two counts of attempted sexual exploitation of a child and one count of sexual exploitation of a child.

that Oliva sent a letter to Vail, confessing to the murder of JonBenét.

An early suspect was Bill McReynolds, who played Santa Claus at private parties for the Ramseys. McReynolds and his wife, Janet, had been at the Ramsey home just two nights before JonBenét was murdered. The police were said to have discovered some eerie parallels between the McReynolds' lives and details in the murder case. On 26 December 1974, the McReynolds' 9-year-old daughter and another girl were abducted by an unknown assailant, who molested the second girl. Within hours, both girls were set free. Additionally, police found out that Janet had written a play in 1977 that was about the torture and murder of 16-year-old Sylvia Likens, who just so happened to be found dead in a basement, much like JonBenét. McReynolds staunchly denied any involvement, and investigators ruled him out.

An electrician named Michael Helgoth worked near the Ramsey home, and had a history of violence and sexual abuse. In November 1996, Helgoth supposedly told a colleague that he and a friend would soon make a large sum of money – $50,000 to $80,000 each. On February 13th, 1997, DA Alex Hunter announced in a press conference that they were narrowing down the list of suspects, until only one would remain. Two days later, Helgoth was found dead by apparent suicide.

In 2006, ex-schoolteacher John Mark Karr spun investigators a lurid tale of how he had drugged and sexually assaulted JonBenét before accidentally killing her. However, his confession conflicted with the evidence, as the autopsy revealed no drugs. Karr's DNA did not match any found on the body, and he was dropped as a suspect.

## AN ENDURING MYSTERY

The tragic case of JonBenét Ramsey divided the nation, with both the police and the public either believing that an intruder broke into the Ramsey home and killed JonBenét, or that she was murdered by a family member. Thanks to the combination of a contaminated crime scene, a bungled initial police investigation, and the diametrically opposed opinions of numerous experts, a definitive solution to the murder of JonBenét Ramsey seems as elusive as ever.

**Michael Helgoth** was the favourite suspect of the Ramseys' private investigator, Ollie Gray.

Karr's ex-wife claimed that he had been with her in **Alabama** at the time of the murder.

In 2016, it was announced that the **DNA** portion of the investigation would be reopened.

# DRIVE-BY SHOOTINGS

**Rap megastars Tupac Shakur and Biggie Smalls were friends who became the bitterest of rivals. Their deaths sparked the most infamous murder mystery in hip-hop history...**

Tupac Shakur and Biggie Smalls were two of the leading rap artists of the 1990s and remain among the most influential of all time. Their staggering fame and success was rapidly rising – until both were killed in drive-by shootings. On 7 September 1996, Tupac Shakur, aged just 25, was gunned down in his car in Las Vegas and died from his wounds six days later. Just months later, on 9 March the following year, 24-year-old Christopher Wallace, better known as Biggie Smalls or The Notorious B.I.G., was shot dead in his car outside a Los Angeles party. The investigations that followed would reveal a grim insight into gang rivalries, greed for money and dangerous grudges.

Tupac and Biggie were key players in the East Coast-West Coast hip-hop rivalry. This was principally between the competing record labels Bad Boy Records (owned by Sean Combs, a.k.a. Puff Daddy) and Death Row Records (owned by Marion "Suge" Knight). The feud sparked bitter tension between rappers, fans and LA gangs, with the Crips backing Bad Boy Records and the Bloods backing Death Row Records. Tupac and Biggie had been friends early in their careers.

*Opposite page, clockwise from top:* Tupac Shakur performs onstage in March 1994 in Chicago, Illinois; The Notorious B.I.G., a.k.a. Biggie Smalls, outside his mother's house in Brooklyn, New York City; CEO of Death Row Records Marion Suge Knight at Los Angeles Superior Court, following the hearings on the murder of Tupac Shakur.

2 VICTIMS | 2 SHOOTINGS

3 KEY SUSPECTS | UNKNOWN WITNESSES

DAI
http://www.mostnewyork.com
NEW

THE
B.I.G.
STEEL

Thou
line Brooklyn
y goodbye
ie Smalls

STORIES ON

Thousands lin
streets to say g
to rapper Big

However, in 1994 Shakur was ambushed and shot five times in Manhattan, and he accused Biggie of being involved in it. Some say it was this incident that launched the rift that would ultimately claim the lives of both artists. Following various accusations, Biggie responded by releasing songs with veiled references to the shooting, while Shakur released "Hit 'Em Up", the lyrics of which bragged that he had slept with Biggie's wife, the singer and songwriter Faith Evans.

## THE MURDER OF TUPAC

On 7 September 1996, Tupac attended the Mike Tyson vs. Bruce Seldon boxing match at the MGM Grand in Las Vegas. After they left, Suge Knight drove Shakur to a party at Club 662, with the rest of Tupac's entourage following in cars behind them. When Knight stopped at a traffic light, a white Cadillac pulled up alongside their black BMW, and more than a dozen shots were fired from a .40 Glock 22 semiautomatic pistol, mortally wounding Tupac and grazing Knight's head. Tupac had been hit twice in the chest, once in the arm and once in the thigh.

# 13 September 1996 / Tupac Shakur dies from his injuries.

The police investigation into Tupac's murder was plagued by a lack of evidence and fearful, uncooperative witnesses. Despite the fact that numerous people were nearby when the shooting occurred, apparently nobody saw a thing. A friend of Tupac's who had been there that night, Yaki Kadafi, said that he could identify the assailant. Unfortunately, he was accidentally shot dead just two months after Tupac, before the police were able to interview him about the case.

The first person of interest in the shooting was a Southside Crips gang member named Orlando Anderson, who had been seen fighting with Tupac in the MGM Grand lobby shortly before the shooting. Suge Knight's friend, Travon Lane, had identified Anderson as the person who had robbed him of his Death Row Records chain a few weeks earlier. Tupac and other members of Death Row Records promptly beat Anderson up. When Tupac was ambushed in a drive-by shooting later

**Nobody** was ever charged for the 1994 shooting of Tupac.

**Tupac Shakur** came from a political background. His mother, Afeni, was a member of the radical Black Panther Party.

**15 minutes** before the shooting, Knight was stopped by Metro patrol cops for playing the car stereo too loudly and for not having licence plates. He was not cited, and was released.

**A Death Row Records** chain was worn by members of the label.

**Orlando Anderson** died in a gang shooting unrelated to the Tupac case in 1998.

that night, Anderson naturally became the prime suspect. He was arrested and questioned on 2 October 1996, but police released him without charge two days later.

## THE MURDER OF BIGGIE

The music world reeled with grief following the shooting of Tupac, but it would not be long before fans were mourning another shocking murder. At around 12:35 a.m. on 9 March 1997, Biggie Smalls climbed into the passenger's seat of his GMC Suburban. He was leaving a Soul Train Awards afterparty hosted by *Vibe* magazine at the Petersen Automotive Museum in Los Angeles. As the car came to a halt at a red light, a dark green (or black, depending on the witness) Chevy pulled up alongside. At least seven rounds from a 9mm pistol of unknown make were fired though the door of Biggie's car and the closed tinted window, hitting only Biggie. It was clearly an assassination, with the killer having a specific target in mind. Biggie was rushed to nearby Cedars-Sinai Hospital, but was pronounced dead at 1:15 a.m. He had been hit by four bullets. The fatal shot struck his right hip, traveling up to his vital organs, including both his heart and his lungs. Death was almost instantaneous.

Biggie closed his second album, *Life After Death*, with the track, **"You're Nobody (Til Somebody Kills You)".** He was shot dead just weeks before its release.

Biggie had ordered a new, bulletproof Chevrolet Suburban. He was killed **three days** before it arrived.

# "BIGGIE HAD TO BE CRAZY TO BE SO UNPROTECTED, IN LOS ANGELES, SIX MONTHS AFTER TUPAC."
LAPD OFFICER

According to witnesses, the **driver** of the car the shots came from was wearing a blue suit and bow tie.

This professional drive-by hit mirrored the earlier slaying of Tupac Shakur and the LAPD soon announced that, in their opinion, the murder was motivated by revenge. "The conventional wisdom is, you know, it's got to be payback for Tupac," an officer commented.[1] Many rap aficionados agreed that the murders were a result of the long-running feud between the East Coast and West Coast, while others speculated that the feud could be a veil to hide a more complex motivation.

## TUPAC SHAKUR SHOOTING

**A** Tupac arrives at Luxor Hotel

**B** 8:00 p.m. Mike Tyson-Bruce Seldon fight at MGM Grand

**C** 8:30-9:00 p.m. Altercation between Tupac and Anderson

**D** Tupac & Suge Knight travel towards Club 662

**E** 11:15 p.m. Shots fired at Tupac and Knight's car

**F** Bullet holes

**G** Suge Knight makes U-turn back towards Las Vegas Blvd.

## BIGGIE SMALLS SHOOTING

**A** Approx 12:35 a.m. Biggie leaves the Soul Train Awards afterparty

**B** Shots fired at Biggie's car

**C** 1:15 a.m. Biggie is pronounced dead at Cedars-Sinai Hospital

**D** Bullet holes

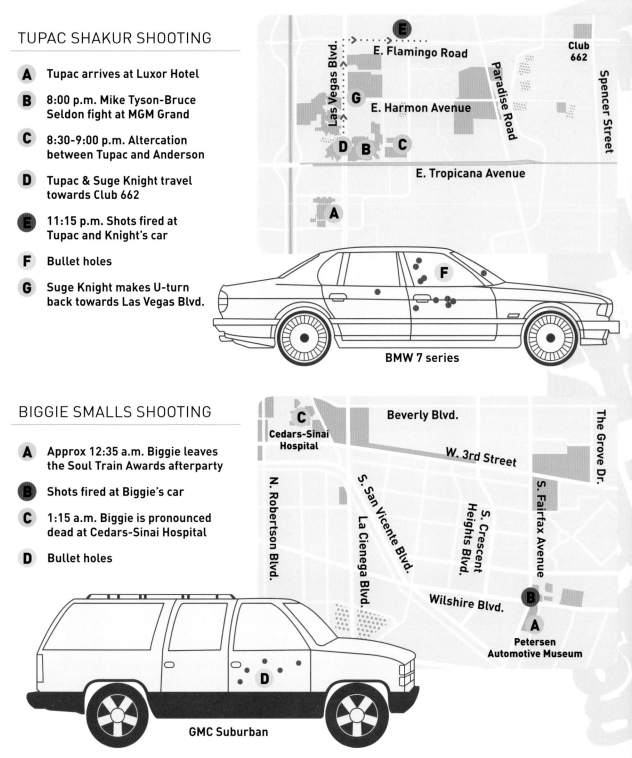

BMW 7 series

GMC Suburban

144

**Far left:** The murder of Tupac Shakur – *Daily News* front page, dated 14 September 1996.

**Left:** The funeral of Biggie Smalls – *Daily News* front page, dated 19 March 1997.

## THE ROLE OF SUGE KNIGHT

Nick Broomfield's 2002 feature-length documentary, *Biggie & Tupac*, put forward the case that Suge Knight ordered Tupac's murder because Knight owed the rap star a large sum of money in royalties, and he had heard through the grapevine that Tupac was planning to switch to another record label. According to Broomfield, the murders of both Shakur and Biggie were orchestrated by Suge and then carried out – and covered up – by the LAPD. He alleged that, at the time of the murder, Knight had several LAPD officers on his payroll working as off-duty bodyguards. In the documentary, a former LAPD detective named Russell Poole reports that his own private investigation into Suge Knight's role in the murders of Tupac and Biggie was rebuffed. He believed that his superiors were engaged in a cover-up and resigned from his job. Randall Sullivan, author of *LAbyrinth*,[2] also presented a case against the Death Row Records boss. He claimed that Knight had Biggie murdered to maintain the illusion of a tit-for-tat feud and divert suspicion from himself for Tupac's murder.

Broomfield also alleged that **Suge Knight** had Tupac killed in order to sell more posthumous albums.

145

# "IF THIS HAD BEEN SOME ORDINARY DRIVE-BY SHOOTING BY SOME INEXPERIENCED GANG-BANGERS, WE WOULD'VE SOLVED IT A LONG TIME AGO."

FORMER LAPD DETECTIVE RUSSELL POOLE

In 2005, Biggie's family filed a wrongful-death lawsuit in which they contended that ex-LAPD officer, David Mack, helped to plan Biggie's shooting. Mack, who by then was serving a 14-year prison sentence for bank robbery, denied any involvement. Kevin Hackie, Tupac's former bodyguard, was called as a witness. He testified that Mack and employees of Death Row Records – including Suge Knight – orchestrated the murder. He stated that he once heard Death Row Records' head of security and LAPD officer Reggie Wright Jr. say that they were going to "get" Biggie in retaliation for Tupac's murder. However, the wrongful-death lawsuit was dismissed.

Suge Knight is currently in **prison** for an alleged hit-and-run murder in 2015 unrelated to the Tupac Shakur and Biggie Smalls cases. His trial date is set for 24 September 2018.

## BIGGIE'S CRIME?

Another widely popular theory is that it was in fact Biggie Smalls who ordered the hit on Tupac Shakur during the escalating East Coast vs. West Coast feud. *Los Angeles Times* reporter Chuck Philips wrote an article in which he claimed that Biggie was in Las Vegas at the time of the shooting and that he supplied the gun and a $1 million bounty for the murder of Tupac, which was carried out by the Crips in revenge for the beating of Orlando Anderson. However, further investigation revealed that Biggie was in a New York recording studio at the time of the murder. Philips would later write another report in which he alleged that Biggie was involved in an earlier shooting of Shakur in New York in 1994. This report claimed that Biggie – along with Sean Combs and Czar Entertainment CEO Jimmy "Henchman" Rosemond – orchestrated the attack in response to perceived disrespect by Tupac. Both Combs and

Rosemond strongly denied any involvement, saying that the "story is beyond ridiculous and is completely false". They added that they had never even been questioned in regard to the shooting.[3] Philips had supposedly received the information from jailhouse informants and in 2011, Dexter Isaac – who was serving time in prison for unrelated crimes – claimed that he had committed the 1994 shooting of Tupac Shakur and that Rosemond had paid him $2,500 to carry it out.

## A MATTER OF DEBT

The conspiracy theories and stream of suspects surrounding the two murder cases are seemingly endless. Retired LAPD homicide detective Greg Kading, who worked on both cases, provided yet another theory. In his 2011 book *Murder Rap: The Untold Story of the Biggie Smalls and Tupac Shakur Murders by the Detective Who Solved Both Cases*,[4] Kading maintains that Sean Combs hired Tupac's assassin for $1 million.

Furthermore, "sources" in a 1998 *Vice* article alleged that Biggie was killed over unpaid debts of $100,000 owed to the Crips, who had been hired as security by Combs. "Puffy refused to pay the hundred thousand. He offered them ten thousand. That's why Biggie Smalls is dead today," said Reggie Wright Jr. (who would later be named as a suspect in the murder of Tupac Shakur by both Suge Knight and then Kevin Hackie during the wrongful-death lawsuit filed by Biggie's family). Combs responded:"That's not even possible. I don't have debts, period."[5]

## GONE BUT NOT FORGOTTEN

The forever-intertwined murders gave an insight into hip-hop's murky underworld. The short lives and violent deaths of Tupac Shakur and Biggie Smalls have made them international icons; few pop culture figures have been mythologised and eulogised to the same extent. Spectacular murals paying tribute to both rap artists adorn streets worldwide. Nevertheless, despite all the many articles, books, movies, and theories devoted to the double murder, nobody has ever been charged with either killing. As long as the key players remain tight-lipped, there is little hope of closure anytime soon.

There were rumors that Tupac had **faked** his own death. These were fuelled by the flood of new songs released following his murder, as well as his posthumous appearances in music videos.

On the night of Biggie's death, his car had been following **Sean Combs' car**, but only Biggie's was stopped at the traffic light.

In 2018, Rapper Keefe D (Duane Keith Davis) claimed in a **deathbed confession** to have been involved in the Tupac shooting.

# SHOT IN BROAD DAYLIGHT

**The brutal murder of television presenter Jill Dando, killed on the doorstep of her London home, was not only headline news because of her celebrity; it truly shocked Britain.**

Jill Dando was a hugely popular BBC TV presenter throughout the 1990s. Her charming personality and warm presence lit up such programmes as *Breakfast News*, the *Six O'Clock News* and the travel series *Holiday*. However, Jill was best known as one of the principal anchors of the prime-time investigative show *Crimewatch*. Each week, Jill would present the key facts of a recent, unsolved UK crime and invite viewers to help police by contacting a special phone number. *Crimewatch* was partly responsible for bringing a number of criminals to justice. Just 37 years old, Jill was in the prime of her life and career, and soon to be married to gynaecologist Alan Farthing.

Alan lived in Bedford Close in the affluent district of Chiswick, West London. Jill was in the process of selling her two-storey home at 29 Gowan Avenue in nearby Fulham so that she could move in with her fiancé. Her own home was up for sale, but she still needed to stop off there to pick up mail and check her fax machine.

On the morning of 26 April 1999, Jill Dando set off to make just such a visit. On the way, she went into a BP garage, bought a new fax machine cartridge and paper, and two fillets of Dover sole. Her image

***Opposite page, clockwise from top:*** Barry George, who was acquitted in 2008 of the murder of Jill Dando; a 1999 police E-fit of a man they wished to interview in connection with the crime; a CCTV image of Jill shopping shortly before her death; TV presenter Jill Dando as the British public knew her.

was captured on security cameras at the garage, and there was no evidence that she was being followed. Jill was scheduled to read the BBC *Six O'Clock News* the following day. In a tragic twist of fate, her own murder would be the lead story.

## FINAL MOMENTS

At approximately 11:30 a.m., Jill arrived at her front door. She was carrying a shopping bag in one hand and her house keys in the other. Before she had a chance to open the door, she was seized, pushed to the ground and shot once in the head.

Jill's neighbour, Richard Hughes, later told police that around the time of the attack, he heard her let out a "very distinctive scream" adding that she sounded "quite surprised".[1] Moments later, he spotted a clean-shaven, well-dressed man with dark hair running down the street. He estimated that the man was in his late 30s or early 40s and was about 1.8 metres (5 ft 11 in) tall. Unaware that anything was awry, Hughes continued with his day.

Fifteen minutes later, a woman passing by discovered Jill lying on the ground outside her home in a pool of blood, her head resting against her front door. She was rushed to Charing Cross Hospital, but was pronounced dead on arrival.

The autopsy revealed that the gun had been pressed hard against Jill's head when it was fired. The impression of the weapon's barrel and sight was clearly visible. A single 9mm bullet had entered just behind the top of her left ear and exited above the right ear, embedding itself in the front door. The gun had not been fitted with a silencer but, because it was fired while forced against Jill's head, the noise of the shot would have been greatly reduced. Damage to the lower part of the door indicated that the victim had been in a crouched position when the fatal shot was fired – presumably forced to the ground by her killer. A bruise on Jill's forearm could have been caused by her assailant.

Police investigators, some of whom had worked alongside Jill on *Crimewatch*, now had the grim task of trying to identify and catch her killer. Speculation immediately focused on the motive for the murder.

**Jill Dando** was voted BBC Personality of the Year in 1997.

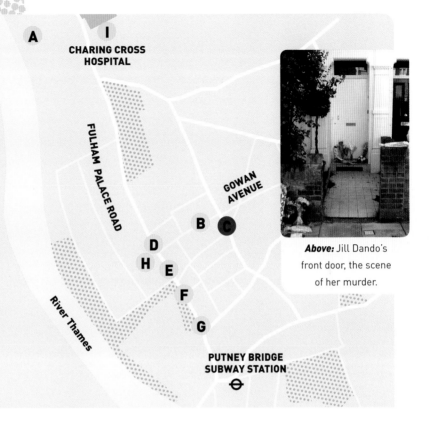

**Above:** Jill Dando's front door, the scene of her murder.

## JILL DANDO'S LAST DAY

**A** 10:00 a.m. Jill leaves fiancé's home

**B** 10:30 a.m. Cleaner sees man outside Jill's house

**C** 11:30 a.m. Jill is shot near to her front door

**D** Witnesses see man running away

**E** Man runs across Fulham Palace Rd

**F** Witnesses see man crouched near Bishops Park, talking on a mobile phone

**G** 11:45 a.m. Man resembling E-fit image takes bus from Fulham Palace Rd to Putney Bridge tube station

**H** 11:52 a.m. Metallic blue Range Rover speeds south down Fulham Palace Rd

**I** 1:03 p.m. Jill dies in hospital

As an investigative journalist and presenter, Jill had come into contact with a number of unsavoury characters over the course of her career. Could she have been targeted by a professional hitman? Was someone seeking revenge? One theory was that she had been murdered by a Yugoslavian or Serbian assassin after making a TV appeal for Kosovo-Albanian refugees, who had been driven from their homes by militias backing Serbian leader Slobodan Milosevic. Another theory was that she had been targeted by a criminal she had helped to expose on an episode of *Crimewatch*. The fact that the killer knew to place the gun directly against her head to minimise noise and blood spatter indicated that he or she could have been a professional.

Another early line of enquiry examined the possibility that Jill had been murdered by an obsessive stalker – an occupational hazard for those in the limelight. "It could either be a stalker or a hitman. However, there are many theories to be explored and nothing will be left untouched," announced Detective Chief Inspector Hamish Campbell, who was leading the investigation.[2]

# 25 May 2000 / Police arrest local man
# Barry George for the murder of Jill Dando.

Massive media coverage meant that the police were under great pressure to find the killer. Nevertheless, their enquiries proved fruitless until, more than a year later, came the announcement the press and public had waited for: Barry George, 39, described as a "local weirdo" with an obsession for Freddie Mercury of the rock band Queen[3], was charged with Jill Dando's murder.

George had come to the attention of the police when he called them shortly after Jill's death to report that he had seen a truck acting suspiciously near her home on the day of the murder. Police discovered that George, who was unemployed, had a history of stalking women and also convictions for sexual assault. He was put under surveillance as police collected evidence against him.

After his arrest, much was made of George's local reputation

Jill Dando's appeal on behalf of Kosovan-Albanian refugees occurred on 6 April 1999, just **20 days** before her murder.

Detectives allegedly assigned an **undercover policewoman** to talk to George, hoping he would confess to the murder, but without success.[4]

as a "loner" and an "oddball". He certainly had obsessive aspects to his personality; he had an unusual interest in celebrities and frequently adopted their names. In the years leading up to his arrest, he had called himself Steve Majors, after stuntman Lee Majors, who played Col. Steve Austin in the TV action series *The Six Million Dollar Man*, as well as Barry Bulsara (Freddie Mercury's real surname). George also fabricated stories about his past, claiming to have been a roadie for Michael Jackson and to have served in the British Army's elite SAS corps. Those who knew him said that he was obsessed with his health and could frequently be seen jogging or cycling in the neighbourhood. Shortly before his trial, George, who had an IQ of just 75, placing him in the lowest 5 percent of the population, was diagnosed with Asperger's syndrome.

George began calling himself **Barry Bulsara** after Freddie Mercury's death in 1991.

George claimed to be **Freddie Mercury's cousin** and pestered women who worked for Queen's fanclub.

In 1983, George wa arrested in the grounds of **Kensington Palace**. He was wearing a balaclava and carrying a knife and rope.

## JUST A FAN?

During Barry George's trial, the prosecution stressed the fact that when his flat in nearby Crookham Road was searched, they discovered 54 newspaper clippings dating back to 1990 about Jill. However, Barry's lawyer, Michael Mansfield QC, pointed out that George also had a number of newspaper clippings concerning other celebrities. In fact, the articles about Jill represented only 8 percent of the clippings found in his flat. "There would be no way of telling from the 670 newspapers [found there] whether he was more interested in Manchester United than Jill Dando, would there?"[5] he said, in response to the prosecution's claim that George was an obsessive fan. "The fundamental flaw in this argument is that there is no evidence, none at all, that, prior to Jill Dando's murder, this defendant had any exaggerated, special, or particular interest in her," Mansfield observed.[6] He emphasised that when Barry's flat was searched, no personal photographs or videos of Jill were found and neither were any autographs. If George was obsessed with Jill, as the prosecution claimed, then he would surely have gone to her house – which was just a short distance from his own – to take photographs of her or at least attempt to ask her for her autograph.

A witness at the trial claimed to have seen George outside Dando's house several hours before the murder; however, the only piece of concrete evidence that could conceivably tie George to the crime was a tiny trace of a substance, reported to be firearm residue, found in the pocket of his jacket. A polyester fibre found on Jill Dando's coat could have come from George's trousers, but the fibre was too common and too small for forensics expert Geoffrey Roe to be sure.

Mansfield went on to claim that the murder could have been a Serbian death squad reprisal for the RAF's bombing of a Belgrade TV station. He also produced an official report that stated that a Serbian warlord had put the BBC director general, Sir John Birt, on a hit list. He suggested to the court that the target may have changed to Jill Dando after security was allegedly stepped up to protect Birt.

A **witness** reported seeing a man matching a police E-fit photograph leaving Jill Dando's street shortly after the murder.

## 2 July 2001 / Barry George is found guilty and sentenced to life in prison.

Despite the flimsy and highly circumstantial evidence against him, Barry George was found guilty. An appeal against the conviction was turned down the following year. Doggedly protesting his innocence, George took the case to the Criminal Cases Review Commission. Forensic science experts now questioned whether the particle found in George's jacket was firearm residue after all. They decided that "it was, in fact, no more likely that the particle had come from a gun fired by George than that it had come from some other source". A retrial was scheduled, and the firearm evidence – so crucial to George's original conviction – was dismissed by the judge.

## 1 August 2008 / Barry George is acquitted of Jill Dando's murder after serving seven years in prison.

Following Barry George's acquittal, there was widespread criticism in the media that the police had focused all their attention on trying to prove George's guilt and devoted insufficient time to investigating other potential suspects. According to reports released in 2015, over 100 possible suspects in the murder were never successfully traced by police. These documents showed that some of these individuals included members of the Serbian secret service and of the IRA, as well as a notorious British gangster based in Spain. Furthermore, 11 men spotted on Jill's street that afternoon were never identified. "I find it disturbing there were a hundred suspects who were never followed up. To put Barry George in the frame, they had to exclude everyone else," said Michael Mansfield.

# "THIS WAS A PROFESSIONAL HIT."

MICHAEL MANSFIELD, Q.C.

After this information came to light, Alice Beers, a BBC colleague of Jill Dando and a former presenter of the *Watchdog* consumer advice program came forward to report that Jill had received threatening letters just weeks before she was killed. She said that both she and Jill had received letters from somebody threatening to kidnap and rape them. She expected the police to contact her about the letters, but no call ever came. "If no stone was left unturned... then I would have been called," she said.[7]

## COPYCAT KILLING

Was Jill Dando's murderer an obsessive fan, a vengeful gangster, or a Serbian hitman? In 2009, the BBC revealed that shortly after Jill's murder, an anonymous caller claiming to have killed Jill Dando had also threatened the head of BBC news at the time, Tony Hall.

In 2012, the Serbian angle seemed to become more plausible when the *Daily Mail* newspaper reported that a Serbian woman, Branka Prpa, claimed that her TV presenter husband, Slavko Curuvija, a critic of Slobodan Milosovic, had been murdered in a similar fashion.[8]

Despite intense media coverage in the press and on television, and a hefty reward for information leading to a conviction, Jill Dando's killer has never been brought to justice.

**Slavko Curuvija** was murdered just 15 days before Jill Dando.

155

# STAIRCASE OF DEATH

**A brutal murder? A tragic accident? A bizarre bird strike? The mysterious fate of successful businesswoman Kathleen Peterson whipped up a storm of bitter controversy and wild theorizing that has never abated.**

To the outside world, the Petersons had everything: a beautiful home, a loving marriage and successful careers. Kathleen Peterson earned a six-figure salary with a telecommunications company. Her husband, Michael, was a full-time novelist. This idyllic image was shattered when, in December 2001, Kathleen was found dead at the bottom of a now-infamous staircase in the couple's North Carolina home. The investigation that followed uncovered lies, adultery and financial woes – and another death at the bottom of a different staircase. It all led to Michael's eventual conviction, but some believe there's an altogether different explanation for Kathleen's death.

Kathleen, 48, and Michael, 58, had both been married before when they met in the mid-1980s. Their meeting was facilitated by their children, who were friends. Kathleen had a teenage daughter named Caitlin. Michael had two sons, Clayton and Todd, from his first marriage, as well as two adopted daughters, named Margaret and Martha.

In 1992, this Brady Bunch-style family moved into a sprawling home on Cedar Street in Durham, North Carolina. Five years later, Michael

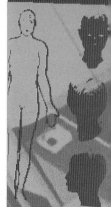

**Opposite page, clockwise:** DA Jim Hardin holds up a photo of murder victim Kathleen Peterson at her husband Michael's 2003 trial; Michael Peterson speaks to reporters after agreeing to an "Alford plea"; SBI agent Duane Deaver explains his blood spatter test to the court; the prosecution compares Kathleen Peterson's injuries with those of Elizabeth Ratliff.

1 VICTIM | 1 KEY SUSPECT

Peterson- Injuries

Ratliff- Injuries

Kathleen Hunt Atwater Peterson

Elizabeth Ann McKee Ratliff- Inj

and Kathleen exchanged vows, making their union official. Caitlin described them as "the most ideal parents".[1]

After moving into the Cedar Street home, Michael started writing columns on city politics for the local newspaper, *The Herald-Sun*. His increased public profile prompted him to run for mayor—a bid that ended badly following revelations that he had exaggerated his military record. He had claimed he was awarded a Purple Heart after being wounded by shrapnel in Vietnam. In reality, he was awarded the medal after he had been hurt in a car accident. Despite this embarrassment, Michael still hoped to enter the political arena. In 2001, a few months before Kathleen's death, he ran for City Council, but again, lost. When officials moved so quickly to charge him with his wife's murder, he wondered if local politics had something to do with it.

## A DESPERATE HUSBAND

In the early hours of 9 December 2001, Michael frantically called 911. "My wife had an accident. She's still breathing," he cried. "She fell down the stairs. She's still breathing, please come."[2] Police and medics arrived, but the scene was not as they expected. Michael had said he spent three hours by the pool that night. Yet, although the temperature outside was only around 12.7°C (55°F), all he was wearing were shorts and a T-shirt. Kathleen was lying in a pool of blood at the foot of the stairs. Blood spatter climbed the walls and reached the ceiling. Then came the autopsy findings: Kathleen's head had been sliced open in places. The medical examiner determined that she had died as the result of a beating, not a fall down the stairs.

# 11 December 2001 / Michael Peterson is charged with his wife Kathleen's murder.

Michael insisted he was innocent. He said that he and Kathleen had been drinking, and that she had also taken a Valium. He could only surmise that the combination of the drug with alcohol made her unsteady on her flip flop-clad feet, causing her to tumble down the

**The Peterson's house** was 10,000 sq. ft. (3,048 sq. m.), had 14 rooms and was white with black shutters.

The **Purple Heart** is a decoration reserved for military personnel injured or killed in action.

There appeared to be a **shoe print** in blood on the back of Kathleen's sweatshirt. Michael was barefoot when police arrived—his sneakers and socks were found next to Kathleen's body

There was a drop of blood on the **inside** of Michael's shorts.

Kathleen was wearing sweatpants and a sweatshirt—appropriate clothing for the **outside** temperature.

wooden staircase. "I've whispered her name more than 1,000 times, and I can't stop crying. I would have never done anything to hurt her," Michael told reporters outside the Durham County Jail.[3]

Prosecutors didn't buy it. While they did find alcohol in Kathleen's system, the blood alcohol content was only 0.07 percent – below the legal limit to drive in North Carolina. Investigators learned that she had suffered from headaches and dizziness for weeks before her fall and had even lost her vision for a half-hour at one point. Nevertheless, they claimed to have found too much evidence that pointed to Michael as the culprit – including another dead body.

## LOOK TO THE PAST

Sixteen years before Kathleen was found dead, a 43-year-old woman named Elizabeth Ratliff died in similar fashion. Ratliff was an American working as a teacher at an airbase near Frankfurt, Germany. She was also a friend of Michael's, who lived in Germany for a spell with his first wife and two sons. On 25 November 1985, Ratliff died after falling down the stairs. As in Kathleen's case, there was a lot of blood at the scene. "The blood was all the way up the staircase," said her friend, Cheryl Appel-Schumacher, who later helped to clean up.[4] The authorities had accepted that the death was an accident and that Elizabeth had suffered a brain haemorrhage while climbing the stairs. Michael helped to organise Elizabeth's funeral and subsequently adopted her daughters.

When North Carolina prosecutors heard of Michael's proximity to another staircase-related death, they announced that the similarities were too many to be coincidental. "Here I have two cases. Two women that appeared to die the same way. Two women that are associated with Michael Peterson. Lightning don't strike the same place twice," Detective Art Holland told a television reporter.[5] Elizabeth's body was exhumed in Texas, and a medical examiner from North Carolina performed a new autopsy. Her verdict: Elizabeth had been beaten to death and the German authorities had overlooked the evidence.

Jim Hardin, the district attorney who prosecuted Peterson, did a great deal of research into the suspect, a lot of which was severely

Michael said that he and Kathleen had been drinking champagne to **celebrate** a possible movie deal for one of his novels.

Michael claimed to have been relaxing by the **pool**, too far away to hear any screams from the house.

The prosecution suggested that the death of his friend **Elizabeth Ratliff** had given Michael the idea of how to murder his own wife and get away with it.

damning. The couple had $143,000 in credit card debt, nearly equal Kathleen's annual salary. In addition, Kathleen was insured for $1.4 million, which Michael would pocket if her death were accidental.[6] Hardin presented a compelling argument that this sum would solve Michael's financial problems and allow him to "continue to live the affluent, privileged life to which he had been accustomed"[7].

Kathleen had confided in her sister, Candace, that her company's stock was in freefall, and that she had lost **$1 million** on paper.

# "FROM WHAT WE'VE FOUND, EVERY ASPECT OF MIKE PETERSON'S LIFE IS A LIE."

JIM HARDIN

However, there was another revelation that prosecutors proffered as the most likely murder motive – Michael had been emailing men to solicit sex and had a cache of gay pornography on his computer. Michael had been emailing a man named Brent Wolgamott for sex. Wolgamott testified that he had exchanged about 20 emails with Michael and talked to him on the phone between 30 August and 5 September 2001. He had planned to meet Michael for a rendezvous, but he stood Michael up and never heard from him again. Wolgamott testified that Michael made it clear he was committed to his wife.

Wolgamott said he charged men **$150** an hour to do "anything under the sun"[8].

State computer experts determined that someone had **deleted** hundreds of gay pornography files in the days leading up to Kathleen's death—and the day after she died.

"If it's an idyllic relationship in this marriage, why is he emailing somebody else to meet for sexual relations outside of marriage?" asked Assistant District Attorney David Saacks.[9] He suggested that Kathleen could have found the pornographic photos or the sex-soliciting emails on Michael's computer and confronted him, which would have been a clear motive for Michael to murder her.

## BLOOD AND THE BLOW POKE

Hardin pointed to the abundance of blood at the scene as proof Michael was lying about Kathleen's fate. During the 2003 trial, the prosecutor called to testify Duane Deaver, a State Bureau of Identification (SBI) agent deemed by Judge Orlando Hudson to be an expert in blood spatter evidence. Deaver told jurors that he had conducted a series of experiments that pointed away from Kathleen having accidentally fallen and towards a beating. Michael's lawyers presented their own blood-spatter expert: Dr Henry Lee asserted that the blood in the stairwell was, in fact, consistent with a fall. Once Kathleen hit her head, she could have coughed up blood while dazed and staggering. Lee went even further by insisting the amount of blood *precluded* a beating.

No murder weapon was found at the scene, but prosecutors offered one anyway. Kathleen's sister Candace had given her a fireplace blow poke as a Christmas gift in 1984. According to pathologist Dr Deborah Radisch, the 101.6-cm (40 in) brass tool was the perfect instrument for inflicting the lacerations found on Kathleen's scalp. The blow poke was found – covered with dead bugs and cobwebs – in a garage during the trial. Hardin questioned a detective who had searched the garage, subtly suggesting that the blow poke had been planted there.

*Right:* A paramedic shows the jury how Michael Peterson was holding his wife's body.

## THE MAIN FLOOR

**A** Kathleen Peterson's body

**B** Staircase

**C** Utility room

**D** Kitchen

**E** Front door

**F** Library/office

## THE FIGHT GOES ON

On 10 October 2003, jurors sided with the prosecution. Michael was sentenced to life in prison without the possibility of parole. His adopted daughters – whose mother's death had been used to prove Michael's guilt – sobbed in the courtroom, certain of his innocence. Kathleen's family – including her daughter Caitlin, who had split with her siblings-by-marriage in believing Michael guilty – applauded the conviction.

Michael's lawyers kept fighting. Throughout the investigation, they had cooperated with a film crew who produced *The Staircase*, a groundbreaking French television documentary that generated worldwide interest in Michael's case. Two days after the conviction, they started the appeal process, arguing that evidence connected with Elizabeth's death never should have been admitted. They challenged Deaver's testimony and qualifications, arguing that he had exaggerated his credentials during the trial. Their objections fell on deaf ears until 2011, when the agent was fired from the SBI for failing to report blood test results that helped lead to the wrongful murder conviction of an innocent man named Greg Taylor, who spent almost 17 years in prison.

Paulette Sutton, a nationally recognised expert in blood pattern analysis, testified that Deaver's methods were antiquated and unscientific. According to an Associated Press story, she "chuckled as she watched videos of [Deaver] beating a Styrofoam head and blood-soaked sponge in an attempt to recreate the blood splatters found on Peterson's shoes and in the stairwell". Sutton's testimony helped overturn Michael's conviction and in 2011, Judge Hudson ruled that Deaver had misled jurors – and that Michael would get a new trial.

Michael spent eight years in prison proclaiming his innocence—but prosecutors still insisted on his guilt. In 2017, facing the prospect of a trial at 73 years old, Michael entered an Alford plea to a manslaughter charge. The plea is treated as a guilty plea for sentencing purposes, but Michael received less than the eight years he had already served. This meant he could walk away a free man. Michael said that taking the Alford plea was the most difficult thing he had ever done, but he believed police and prosecutors "would do anything to convict me. And I am not

Caitlin and her father were awarded the $1.4 million **life insurance** policy for which Michael had been the beneficiary.

The documentary series *The Staircase* was directed by Oscar winner Jean-Xavier de Lestrade. It won a prestigious **Peabody Award** in 2005.

An audit found that, over Deaver's 25-year career, he had **falsified evidence** in 34 separate cases.

The Alford plea allowed Michael to maintain his innocence while acknowledging that there was **enough evidence** to convict him of the charge.

going to put my life and my freedom in their hands"[10]. Prosecutors considered the plea a win. Durham District Attorney Roger Echols stated: "It has always been, and remains today, the State's position that Michael Peterson is responsible for the death of Kathleen Peterson."[11]

## OWL ATTACK?

*The Staircase* documentary unwittingly recruited armchair detectives worldwide to proffer theories explaining what could have happened to Kathleen that night. Most are split between the two scenarios presented at trial: that either Michael killed his wife, or she fell in a manner that caused multiple injuries to her head.

However, the most intriguing theory suggests the case is more a "hoo-dunn-it" than a whodunnit. In 2003, Larry Pollard, a friend of Michael's, asked prosecutors to reopen the case because of information that pointed to another culprit altogether: an owl. Looking at autopsy photos, Pollard said that some of the gashes on Kathleen's body looked like marks from an owl's exceptionally sharp talons. Pollard consulted with ornithological experts who agreed that the pattern and shape of the cuts on Kathleen's head looked far more like an owl attack than a fireplace tool.

Hardin dismissed this theory as being completely ridiculous, but owl attacks are not as outlandish as they might seem. Kate Davis, executive director of a wild bird education organisation in Florence, Italy, said raptors are known to get aggressive when defending their nests and hatchlings. They tend to attack at night; Michael's phone call to 911 was at 2:40 a.m. Kathleen was holding clumps of her own hair, mixed with wood splinters and needles from a cedar tree. Could an owl have become entangled in her hair?

When the SBI eventually acknowledged finding a "microscopic feather" on a clump of hair in Kathleen's hand, Pollard shouted: "The feather has been found!"[12] With Michael's plea agreement, however, the Owl Theory will never have its day in court. Michael himself said he has run out of theories: "The only thing I know absolutely, positively, is that I had nothing to do with Kathleen's death."[13]

Some thought that Kathleen may have interrupted an **intruder**, who pummeled her before fleeing.

The species of owl put forward as Kathleen's potential attacker is a **barred owl**. An adult weighs 725 g (1.6 lb), with a wingspan up to 112 cm (44 in).

Kathleen may have been attacked by the owl **outside** and then staggered in and collapsed at the foot of the stairs.

In 2007, Caitlin and Michael reached a $25 million settlement in a wrongful death suit. Caitlin said this ensured that Michael couldn't **write a book** about the case and pocket the profit.

# LOST IN THE MARSHLAND

**The woman was terrified, seemingly running for her life. Soon after she vanished into the night, a peaceful area of rural Long Island began to yield up its terrible secrets.**

**D**ense marshland runs alongside Long Island's Ocean Parkway, a beautiful – albeit desolate – stretch of beach highway. It was here, hidden away from the eyes of passing drivers, that a serial killer disposed of his victims. Over the course of almost 20 years, the Long Island Serial Killer – or the Gilgo Beach Killer, as he was also known – murdered between 10 and 16 people associated with prostitution. The identity of the killer and his motives have perplexed homicide detectives ever since the first discovery of his victims in December 2010, and has led to one of the most infamous, unidentified serial-killer cases in recent history.

This grim story unfolded on May 1 of that year, when Shannan Gilbert, a 24-year-old Craigslist escort from New Jersey, vanished. Before her disappearance, Shannan had visited the home of Joseph Brewer, a resident of the upmarket gated community of Oak Beach, who had hired Shannan as his escort for the evening. Brewer would later tell police that, after arriving at his home, Shannan began to act erratically and appeared disoriented before fleeing out into the warm night. She ran straight past her pimp, Michael Pak, who was waiting

*Opposite page, main image:* Joseph Brewer's house, which Shannan Gilbert fled from.
*Opposite page, clockwise from top:* Police search Jones Beach in April 2011; Ocean Parkway where the killer dumped the bodies; suspect Joel Rifkin; memorial for Melissa Barthelemy; newspaper articles covering the discovery of the bodies.

TOP STORIES

**ot among bodies**

Family's agony goes on

Kin's grief deepens over beach graveyard

School-job
no-Show
ring nailed

**MORE BODIES,
NO SHANNAN**

10 VICTIMS | 2 SUSPECTS

for her outside in his black Ford Explorer. Several neighbours saw – and heard – Shannan that night. She ran down the street of expensive houses, pounding on doors and screaming for help. Despite her evident distress, nobody let her in. Instead, they called 911 and watched as she ran away from the Oak Beach gatehouse towards Anchor Way and then onto the bayou, completely out of sight. Exactly who Shannan was running from remains a mystery. At some point during her escape, she managed to call 911 and hollered: "They're trying to kill me!"[1]

## THE LOST WOMEN

Seven months after Shannan disappeared, four bodies were found close to one another, nestled among the thorny underbrush running alongside Ocean Parkway on Gilgo Beach. As news of this gruesome find circulated in the media, locals and investigators presumed that one of the bodies would be Shannan Gilbert, as the site was just 4.8 km (3 miles) from where she was last seen. However, an examination of the remains concluded that none of them was her. They were identified as Amber Lynn Costello, 27; Melissa Barthelemy, 24; Maureen Brainard-Barnes, 25; and Megan Waterman, 22. Just like Shannan, all four women had been working as Craigslist escorts when they disappeared. Maureen went missing in July 2007 when she left Norwich, Connecticut for New York City; Melissa vanished in July 2009 after meeting with an escort client; Megan disappeared just a month after Gilbert, having placed a Craigslist advertisement; and Amber vanished in September 2010, after arranging to meet a client who offered her $1,500 for her services.

It became clear that these discoveries had unearthed a serial killer's dumping ground and, in April 2011, an extensive search was finally launched. Airplanes fitted with high-tech photographic equipment scoured the area, while police with horses and dogs explored the undergrowth alongside the highway and beach. The search led to the discovery of six more victims approximately 1.6 km (1 mile) east of the other bodies: four more women, a female toddler and an Asian man wearing women's clothing. Of these victims – which were all found within 3.2 km (2 miles) of the first cluster of bodies – only one has ever

Shannan's behaviour led many to believe that she was on drugs or experiencing some kind of **psychotic episode**.

No one knows who Shannan was referring to when she cried out that someone was **trying to kill her.**

**The four bodies** were found wrapped in burlap sacks.

In an effort to help capture the killer, an **online petition** asked authorities to grant immunity to sex workers who came forward with information.

**The toddler** was between 16 and 24 months old and was a non-Caucasian.

been identified: 20-year-old Jessica Taylor. She vanished in July 2003, while working as an escort in Manhattan, New York. Shortly after her disappearance, her dismembered torso had been found in Manorville, New York, around 64.4 km (40 miles) east of Gilgo Beach. Her skull, hands and a forearm were subsequently discovered during the search of Gilgo Beach itself. The remains of another victim, known only as "Jane Doe No. 6", were also found at Manorville and Gilgo Beach. While the police were unable to identify the remains, forensic experts did determine that none belonged to Shannan Gilbert.

**Jane Doe No. 6**
was thought to have been around 5 ft 2 in (1.57 meters) tall and between 18 and 35-years old.

**Ocean Parkway area**
- Length: 15.59 miles (25.09 km)

## REMAINS FOUND

**A** Jessica Taylor's skull, hands, forearms

**B** Asian male

**C** Unidentified child remains, Jane Doe No. 6 remains

**D** Unidentified human bones

**E** Unidentified skull

**F** Amber Lynn Costello, Melissa Barthelemy, Maureen Brainard-Barnes, Megan Waterman

**G** Shannan Gilbert

## WHAT HAPPENED TO SHANNAN?

In early December 2011, an extended search turned up Shannan Gilbert's purse, mobile phone, lip gloss, jeans and shoes in a marsh near Oak Beach, several miles to the east of the second group of bodies. Following the discovery, the search for Shannan intensified, with the outcome looking decidedly bleak. Dozens of officers using machetes and a bulldozer were called to the scene.

# 13 December 2011 / The remains of Shannan Gilbert are found in a shallow marsh near Oak Beach, the place where she was last seen alive.

The authorities soon announced that they believed Gilbert had drowned in the marsh and that her death was not connected to the other murders, despite the fact that she was found in the same vicinity and fit the victim profile. Her family was furious with this conclusion and lambasted this "premature and inconsiderate" theory.[2] In fact, before Gilbert's body was even found, Suffolk County Police Commissioner Richard Dormer publicly announced that he believed Gilbert had wandered off and accidentally drowned. "I think Dormer just wants to find the remains, say she drowned, and close the case before he retires," fumed Mari Gilbert, Shannan's mother.

The investigation also drew criticism from some of the victims' families, who accused officers of incompetence and inaction. Some even hired their own private investigators. Shannan's family hired Michael Baden, a forensic pathologist, in order to obtain a second opinion on her autopsy. According to Baden, there was no evidence that Shannan had died of natural causes, a drug overdose, or, as Suffolk County Police believed, by drowning. He observed that there was insufficient information to determine a definite cause of death, but found that the hyoid bone in Shannon's neck was deformed, which could have been caused by strangulation.[3]

## "THESE STRUCTURES, THE LARYNX AND THE HYOID BONE, ARE OFTEN FRACTURED DURING HOMICIDAL MANUAL STRANGULATION."
MICHAEL BADEN

Since the discovery of the bodies, plenty of theories have abounded. Some have speculated that the killer was a seasonal worker, a drifter or a fisherman from Freeport. More lurid theories have also been put forward – that the killer was making snuff films or belonged to a satanic cult. Another hypothesis involved a local businessman who committed suicide days after Shannan's remains were found. Police were quick to deny that he was a suspect; he was merely a victim of rumours and hearsay.

## UNTRACEABLE CALLS

One of the more likely theories was that the killer was a police officer – or ex-police officer – with extensive knowledge of law enforcement techniques. Following Melissa Barthelemy's disappearance, the Long Island Serial Killer made taunting phone calls to her 16-year-old sister, Amanda. He called Melissa a whore and asked if Amanda knew what Melissa was doing. These calls were always placed from crowded areas such as New York's Penn Station and Madison Square Garden, where it would have been next to impossible for surveillance cameras to single out the caller from the crowd. Moreover, the caller only stayed on the line for under three minutes, indicating that he knew it took from three to five minutes to successfully trace a phone call. Police were convinced that these calls came from the killer, as opposed to a prankster, leading many to believe that the murderer must have been a member of a law enforcement agency at some point in his life.

Amid the investigation into the murders, Suffolk County Police Chief James Burke resigned, adding fuel to the rogue cop theory. Following his resignation, Burke was arrested for a 2012 assault on Christopher Loeb, who had stolen a duffel bag filled with pornography and sex toys from Burke's car. After Burke's arrest, an escort came forward to claim that he was into "rough sex". She alleged that Burke had attempted to strangle her during a party in Oak Beach, the gated community where Gilbert was last seen alive. It then transpired that Burke had stymied an FBI investigation into the Long Island murders and had intentionally kept them out of the loop. What was he afraid of the FBI finding? In 2016, an attorney for Shannan Gilbert's family alleged that there could be a connection between Burke and the murders; however, he was never charged.

## THE LYING DOCTOR

Another suspect in the slayings was Dr Peter Hackett, a physician and neighbour of Joseph Brewer (one of the last people to see Shannan alive). Dr Hackett lived in close proximity to the marshland where Shannan Gilbert's remains would later be found. According to Shannan's mother, Mari Gilbert, Dr Hackett had called her the day after her daughter went missing and told her that he was a doctor who "ran a home for wayward girls". Several days later, Dr Hackett denied he had ever made this call. Phone records, however, confirmed that he had called Mari Gilbert twice following Shannan's disappearance.

In 2012, Shannan's family filed a wrongful death lawsuit against Dr Hackett, in which they alleged that he could have prevented her death. "Dr Hackett told Mari Gilbert that he ran a home for wayward girls, and that Shannan was in his care," said John Ray, an attorney for the Gilbert family. "Why would anyone do something like that?"[4] Dr Hackett was eventually ruled out as a suspect by Suffolk County Police. Joseph Brewer also fell under a cloud of suspicion, since Shannan was last spotted fleeing from his home in a state of panic. However, he, too, was quickly ruled out as a suspect when Suffolk County Police could find no evidence to tie him to any of the murders.

## INVESTIGATOR THEORIES

For years, law enforcement remained tight-lipped on the notorious Long Island Serial Killer, but in 2017, the silence was at last broken. Suffolk County Assistant District Attorney Robert Biancavilla named a new suspect: John Bittrolff, a carpenter who had recently been charged with two 25-years-to-life sentences for beating two sex workers to death in 1993 and 1994. Bittrolff lived in the hamlet of Manorville, where the torsos of two of the Long Island Serial Killer's

On the fifth anniversary of the discovery of the first set of remains, it was announced that the **FBI** would join in on the investigation.

In 2016, Shannan's mother, Mari Gilbert, was **stabbed to death** by her 27-year-old daughter, Sarra Elizabeth Gilbert, who was suffering from schizophrenia.

**A wrongful death lawsuit** is brought by representatives of the deceased's estate. It seeks compensation from the person held to be legally at fault for the deceased's death.

victims were discovered. Biancavilla alleged that some aspects of the evidence found over the years at Ocean Parkway were similar to the earlier crimes attributed to Bittrolff. Evidence found at the crime scenes, however, did not match any found at earlier crime scenes; it was thus impossible to conclusively link Bittrolff to the murders.

A hypothetical profile of the killer was created by Jim Clemente, a criminal profiler; Scott Bonn, an assistant professor of sociology at Drew University; and former Nassau County Assistant District Attorney Fred Klein. They deduced that the killer was likely a white male in his mid-20s to mid-40s; he was married or had a girlfriend; he was intelligent and articulate; he had a decent job that gave him access to burlap sacks and he lived – or once lived – near Ocean Parkway.

A final suspect for at least some of the murders attributed to the Long Island Killer is convicted serial killer Joel Rifkin. Between the years of 1989 and 1993, he murdered at least nine women in New York and Long Island, disposing some of their bodies in the same general area as the Long Island Serial Killer. However, in an interview, Rifkin denied that any of the victims were his. He stated that he dumped his victims "hundreds of miles apart" and not in the same location – something he called the Long Island Serial Killer "sloppy" for doing.[5]

## TELLING THE STORY

On that fateful night of 1 May 2010, Shannan Gilbert drove past the remote marshland where 10 victims of the Long Island Serial Killer lay while en route to an escort call. Unknown to her at the time, the disturbing and mysterious events that would unfold over the forthcoming hours would forever link her to those bodies and spark one of the most extensive murder investigations in Long Island history. Numerous newspapers and magazines; a best-selling book, *Lost Girls: An Unsolved American Mystery* by Robert Kolker;[6] and an episode in the television documentary series *The Killing Season* have all told the story of the 10 bodies discovered along the Ocean Parkway. Despite the extensive media coverage, the case still remains unsolved and open.

# INDEX

# REFERENCES

**The Shrouded House**
1. https://iowacoldcases.org/case-summaries/villisca-axe-murders/
2. *Quad-City Times*, 21 August 1912
3. *Adams County Free Press*, 29 November 1916
4. https://www.smithsonianmag.com/history/the-ax-murderer-who-got-away-117037374/
5. *The Man From the Train: The Solving of a Century-Old Serial Killer Mystery* by Bill James and Rachel McCarthy James (Scribner, 2017)
6. *Quad-City Times*, 16 January 1994
7. *Fort Wayne News*, 3 September 1917

**A Hollywood Whodunit**
1. *King of Comedy* by Mack Sennett, as told to Cameron Shipp (Doubleday, 1954)
2. *Billings Gazette*, 11 February 1922
3. *A Deed of Death: The Story Behind the Unsolved Murder of Hollywood Director William Desmond Taylor* by Robert Giroux (Knopf, 1990)
4. *Washington Times*, 8 February 1922
5. *Los Angeles Times*, 10 February 1922
6. *Murder in Hollywood: Solving a Silent Screen Mystery* by Charles Higham (University of Wisconsin Press, 2004)
7. *Daily News*, 19 September 1957—When Hollywood Was Really Wild
8. *Tinseltown: Murder, Morphine, and Madness at the Dawn of Hollywood* by William J. Mann (Harper, 2014)
9. *William Desmond Taylor* by Bruce Long (The Scarecrow Press, 1991)

**The Bodies in the Barn**
1. http://hinterkaifeck.net/
2. *Abendzeitung*, 17 March 2018

**The Impossible Murder**
1. *Liverpool Echo*, 14 June 2015
2. *Express*, 24 September 2012
3. *Wallace: The Final Verdict* by Roger Wilkes (The Bodley Head, 1984)
4. *The Killing of Julia Wallace: Liverpool's Most Enigmatic and Brutal Murder Finally Solved?* by John Gannon (Amberley Publishing, 2012)

**Deep Waters**
1. *The Advocate*, 15 June 1935
2. *The Shark Arm Murders* by Alex Castles (Wakefield Press 1995)

**Panic in the City**
1. *In the Wake of the Butcher: Cleveland's Torso Murders* by James Jessen Badal (The Kent State University Press/Black Squirrel Books, 2014)
2. *The Daily Times*, 28 January 1957
3. *Muncie Evening Press*, 14 September 1977

**Scandal in Shangri-La**
1. *White Mischief: The Murder of Lord Erroll* by James Fox (Random House, 1983)
2. *Evening Star*, 20 March 1941
3. *The Sunday Times*, 31 January 1999
4. *Evening Star*, 24 March 1941
5. *The Telegraph*, 11 May 2007
6. *The Temptress: the Scandalous Life of Alice, Countess de Janzé* by Paul Spicer (Simon & Schuster, 2010)

**The Skeleton in the Wood**
1. *The Independent*, 14 August 1999

2. *Punt PI*, series 7, "Who Put Bella in the Wych Elm?" (BBC Radio 4)

**Death of a Dreamer**
1. *Los Angeles Times*, 24 January 1947
2. *Los Angeles Times*, 16 January 1947
3. *San Bernadino County Sun*, 19 January 1947
4. *The Pittsburgh Press*, 18 January 1947
5. https://www.biography.com/people/black-dahlia-21117617
6. *Indiana Gazette*, 25 January 1947
7. *Middletown Times Herald*, 30 January 1947
8. *The Encyclopedia of Unsolved Crimes* (2nd ed.) by Michael Newton (Checkmark Books, 2009)
9. *Los Angeles Times*, 11 January 1949
10. https://www.rollingstone.com/culture/features/has-the-black-dahlia-murder-finally-been-solved-w515848
11. *Billings Gazette*, 11 May 2003
12. *Black Dahlia Avenger: A Genius for Murder* by Steve Hodel (Arcade Pub., 2003)
13. http://blackdahlia.web.unc.edu/george-knowlton/

**Did Sam Do It?**
1. *The Weekend Australian*, 17 October 1988
2. *Endure and Conquer: My Twelve-Year Fight for Vindication* by Dr. Sam Sheppard (The World Publishing Company, 1966)
3. *The Columbus Dispatch*, 9 February 1997
4. *Tailspin: The Strange Case of Major Call* by Bernard F. Connors (British American Publishing, 2004)

**The Last Bike Ride**
1. *The Chronicle Herald*, 20 June 2006
2. *Waterloo Region Record*, 29 August 2007
3. *Waterloo Region Record*, 14 February 2007
4. *Guelph Mercury*, 29 August 2007

**Campsite of Horrors**
1. *Hartford Courant*, 17 August 2005
2. *Legend of Bodom* by Ulf Johansson (2016)
3. *Bodmin arvoitus* by Jorma Palo (WSOY, 2003)
4. *MTV3*, 26 August 2005

**Killing for Fun**
1. *Los Angeles Times*, 15 October 1969
2. https://www.biography.com/people/zodiac-killer-236027
3. *San Francisco Chronicle*, 16 November 1970
4. *Zodiac* and *Zodiac Unmasked* by Robert Graysmith (Berkley, 2007)
5. *Chicago Tribune*, 4 March 2007
6. *The Most Dangerous Animal of All* by Gary L. Stewart with Susan Mustafa (Harper, 2014)
7. https://www.sacbee.com/latest-news/article210320689.html

**Stranger Danger**
1. *Detroit Free Press*, 9 January 1977
2. *Detroit Free Press*, 22 January 1977
3. *The News Palladium*, 22 January 1977
4. *Detroit Free Press*, 26 March 1977
5. *The Detroit News*, 19 October 2007
6. https://www.hometownlife.com/story/news/2017/03/19/unsolved-homicides-still-haunt-community-birmingham-farmington-cold-case/

**Death at the Drugstore**
1. http://www.chicagomag.com/Chicago-Magazine/October-2012/Chicago-Tylenol-Murders-An-Oral-History/

2. *Chicago Tribune*, 1 October 1982
3. http://www.chicagomag.com/Chicago-Magazine/October-2012/Chicago-Tylenol-Murders-An-Oral-History/
4. *Chicago Tribune*, 3 October 1982
5. *The Dispatch*, 3 March 1996
6. *Chicago Tribune*, 20 January 2013

**A Christmas Nightmare**
1. *Perfect Murder, Perfect Town* by Lawrence Schiller (HarperTorch, 1999)
2. http://www.statementanalysis.com/jonbenet-ramsey-murder/
3. *The Age*, 24 October 1998
4. *Rolling Stone*, 12 October 2016
5. https://www.intouchweekly.com/posts/jonbenet-murder-case-108441

**Drive-By Shootings**
1. *New York Daily News*, 11 March 1997
2. *LAbyrinth: A Detective Investigates the Murders of Tupac Shakur and Notorious B.I.G.* by Randall Sullivan (Atlantic Monthly Pr, 2002)
3. *Daily Press*, 18 March 2008
4. *Murder Rap: The Untold Story of the Biggie Smalls and Tupac Shakur Murders* by Greg Kading (One Time Publishing, 2011)
5. *Vice*, March 1998

**Shot in Broad Daylight**
1. *Evening Mail*, 27 April 1999
2. *The Independent*, 28 April 1999
3. *Guardian*, 2 August 2008
4. www.mirror.co.uk/news/uk-news/jill-dando-murder-cops-tried-5431123
5. *Associated Press*, 2 July 2001
6. *The Times*, 16 June 2001
7. *The Scotsman*, 30 March 2015
7. http://www.dailymail.co.uk/news/article-2109602

**Staircase of Death**
1. http://www.nbcnews.com/id/15894727
2. https://www.washingtonpost.com/news/arts-and-entertainment/wp/2018/06/11/netflixs-the-staircase-the-long-sensational-murder-trial-behind-the-new-series/
3. *Rocky Mount Telegram*, 8 August 2003
4. http://www.cnn.com/2003/LAW/08/19/ctv.novelist.trial/index.html
5. h/ttp://www.nbcnews.com/id/15894727/ns/dateline_nbc/t/death-bottom-stairs/
6. *Written in Blood* by Diane Fanning (St. Martin's Press, 2005).
7. *Rocky Mount Telegram*, 2 July 2003
8. http://www.cnn.com/2003/LAW/08/12/ctv.novelist.trial/
9. *Rocky Mount Telegram*, 8 August 2003
10. *Asheville Citizen-Times*, 25 Febuary 2017
11. https://www.newsobserver.com/news/local/crime/article134727939.html
12. *The New Journal*, 1 October 2008
13. *Asheville Citizen-Times*, 25 Febuary 2017

**The Bodies in the Marshland**
1. *48 Hours*, 20 July 2013
2. *New York Daily News*, 10 December 2011
3. *The Jersey Journal*, 13 February 2016
4. *Vice*, 3 February 2016
5. *News & Politics Examiner*, 15 April 2011
6. *Lost Girls: An Unsolved American Mystery* by Robert Kolker (Harper, 2013)